HISTORICAL RECORD OF THE 4TH BATTALION 16TH PUNJAB REGIMENT

HISTORICAL RECORD

OF THE

4TH BATTALION 16TH PUNJAB REGIMENT

The Naval & Military Press Ltd

Reproduced by kind permission of the Central Library, Royal Military Academy, Sandhurst

Published by
The Naval & Military Press Ltd
Unit 10, Ridgewood Industrial Park,
Uckfield, East Sussex,
TN22 5QE England
Tel: +44 (0) 1825 749494
Fax: +44 (0) 1825 765701
www.naval-military-press.com

Dedication

THIS BOOK IS DEDICATED TO

ALL RANKS OF THE BATTALION

WHO LAID DOWN THEIR LIVES DURING THE GREAT WAR

1914-1918.

CONTENTS

CHAPTER V

THE 9TH BHOPAL INFANTRY, 1903-1904

CHAPTER VI

1904-1914

PART II.

SERVICE IN FRANCE: 1914-15.

CHAPTER VII

EARLY MEASURES

CHAPTER VIII

NEUVE CHAPELLE, OCTOBER, 1914

CHAPTER IX

FESTUBERT, NOVEMBER, 1914

CHAPTER X

GIVENCHY

CHAPTER XI

SECOND BATTLE OF YPRES

CHAPTER XII

OPERATIONS DURING MAY, 1915

PART III.

SERVICE IN EGYPT.

CHAPTER XIII

PART IV.

SERVICE IN MESOPOTAMIA.

CHAPTER XIV

CHAPTER XV

CHAPTER XVI

CHAPTER XVII

THE CAPTURE OF BAGHDAD

CHAPTER XVIII

OPERATIONS SUBSEQUENT TO THE FALL OF BAGHDAD

CHAPTER XIX

MAY, 1917, TO MARCH, 1919

PART V.

1919 TO 1930.

CHAPTER XX

LIST OF APPENDICES

LIST OF MAPS AND SKETCHES

FOREWORD

PART I of this History was written in 1905 by Major C. C. Jackson, who was killed in action in Mesopotamia, 1915. The original script is in the Officers' Mess, written by him in a very fine copper-plate handwriting. It is regretted that it has not been possible to reproduce the coloured illustrations depicting the old uniforms ; these are, however, described in the text of the book.

Part II was written by Lieutenant-Colonel G. D. Martin, M.C., in 1928. He was an Adjutant of the Battalion during its stay in France in 1914-1915.

Parts III and IV were written by Colonel H. H. Smith, D.S.O., in 1928. He was with the Battalion throughout this period, and from 1916 onwards he commanded the Battalion for the greater part of the time.

All ranks of the Battalion are greatly indebted to these officers for the care and trouble they have taken in writing these parts of the History.

It is regretted that an accurate record has not been kept of the casualties which occurred during the Great War. The War Diaries and Battalion Orders are silent on this point to a large extent. Every time the Battalion went into the trenches there were casualties, which have not been recorded. For this reason mention of casualties, except after the large battles, has not been made.

This History has been continued up to the end of 1930, with the Battalion serving in Chitral. It is hoped to add a fresh chapter to this book after every decade.

DROSH, CHITRAL.

February, 1931.

EVOLUTION OF THE NAME OF THE BATTALION

1818 :
THE BHOPAL CONTINGENT.

|

1859 :
THE BHOPAL LEVY.

|

1865 :
THE BHOPAL BATTALION.

|

1903 :
THE IX BHOPAL INFANTRY.

|

1922 :
THE 4TH BATTALION 16TH PUNJAB REGIMENT.

Part I.

HISTORY: 1818-1914.

CHAPTER I.

THE ORIGIN OF THE CORPS.

EARLY in the eighteenth century the employment of troops belonging to the British Government was necessitated in the Bhopal State and in the surrounding country owing to the disorders engendered by the Pindaras and other freebooters. These latter were not only harrying the immediate district, but even regarded the fastnesses of the Central Indian Plateau very much in the light of a permanent base of operations, where they could mature their plans during the hot weather and succeeding rains in safety and amid a pleasant climate. They were ready to issue forth as soon as the waters of the Nerbudda River had subsided sufficiently to render the selected " ghat " an easy crossing-place, and the first " nip " in the October morning had foretold their expedition, on rapine and plunder bent, would be a pleasantly cool as well as a remunerative one. The Berars and the Deccan had good reason to dread each return of that season of the year " when every prospect pleases " ; the Pindaras took care that the latter portion of the quotation—" and only man is vile "—was amply fulfilled. Accordingly a British force was sent to engage these freebooters, and to strike at the source itself whence the stream of violence and murder issued ; but this force was more in the nature of a temporary expedition than a permanent garrison, and the habits of the Pindaras were too deeply ingrained to be exorcised by one rebuff, severe though temporary. It therefore appeared advisable to have a permanent body of men at the disposal of British authority stationed at some convenient point within Bhopal territory itself.

Central India in 1818.

A Political agency was established in 1818 at Sehore, about twenty-four miles west of the city of Bhopal, on the Siwan, a small tributary of the Parbatti River. Captain Stewart, the Political Officer deputed to inquire into and settle the affairs in those parts, drew up a treaty under which the Nawab of Bhopal undertook to maintain a force of 600 Horse and 400 Infantry for the pacification of the country

Origin of the Regiment, A.D. 1818.

The Bhopal Contingent.

Cavalry and Infantry.

and for the maintenance of law and order. This treaty was duly signed and ratified by the Governor-General in Council. The force was named " The Bhopal Contingent," was located at Sehore, and was definitely under the orders of the resident Political Officer. No British officers appear to have been appointed to the Contingent during the first few years of its existence as a formed body, nor were the full numbers of its cavalry or infantry realized. In all probability the men then serving in the force were drafted, just as they were, from the Nawab's own troops, bringing their arms, accoutrements and uniform, though it is not impossible that the last may have been somewhat nondescript.

A representation of a serious shortage of numbers was made to the Bhopal Durbar by Mr. T. H. Maddock, the then Political Officer, in April, 1824, and in reply thereto a large number of horsemen were sent from the State forces to complete the numbers of the Contingent. As it seemed that the Durbar were somewhat unwilling to forego the services of these horsemen, 300 of them were sent back by Mr. Maddock directly after they had joined the Contingent.

It must be clearly understood that whilst the services of the Contingent were solely at the disposal of the British, the cost of the up-keep of the same was, under treaty obligation, to be defrayed by the Nawab of Bhopal. The unsatisfactory state of affairs related in the foregoing paragraph seems to have been principally caused by the heavy expense thrown on the Bhopal Durbar at a time when the revenue had not realized expectations, and partly by the difficulty in obtaining recruits locally on account of " the repugnance of the Bhopal people to be disciplined or to wear uniform."

First reorganization, 1824. All three arms. First mention of Artillery. British Officers, Suggested Appointment. Extract from Correspondence of 1824.

Accordingly, Mr. Maddock drew up a scheme for the complete reorganization of the Contingent by which a saving would be effected, and under which it was trusted that the men " would be made equal to regular troops in every respect." The brilliant idea of improving military efficiency by cutting expenditure thereon is therefore not entirely confined to politicians of a later date. But the principal changes on which the new reorganization was based were to have fewer mounted men, and to draw the personnel from the robust fighting classes of northern India instead of recruiting locally. The proposed establishment was to consist of 302 cavalry, 674 infantry, and 20 artillery men. The pay of the sepoys was fixed at Rs5 a month, and the various ranks of the Contingent were settled. Mr. Maddock further recommended that " His Lordship in Council will think it necessary to appoint a fit Military Officer to command the Contingent, and bring it into a disciplined state, or little benefit will be derived from the reform." A suggestion was also made that muskets should replace the matchlocks with which the infantry were armed. A very interesting feature in connection with this scheme is the mention of " 4 nishan-bardars " in the cavalry, as the guidons of green silk emblazoned with the " fish," the badge of the regiment, which they carried on parade and which are still in possession of the regiment.

The First British Commandant, 1824.

All the above proposals were sanctioned by the Government in letter No. 234, dated October 15th, 1824. There is, however, considerable doubt as to who was the first British Commandant. Report has it that this was Captain J. Johnson, but this is at least doubtful, as it was clearly stated in a letter written about that time that " Captain Johnson, the only Military Officer in Sehore," could not be spared for duty with the Contingent owing to his other work. Possibly he may have been subsequently appointed notwithstanding this objection ; at all events, traditions of an earlier period connected his name with the Regiment. This, no doubt, was largely from hearsay, and there is no documentary evidence to support it.

Chain Singh, Rajah of Narsingh Garh, 1824.

There is no very accurate record of what duties were performed by the Contingent in its early days, though reference is frequently made to it in old files of correspondence in the office of the Political Agent in Bhopal. Escorts were furnished for various Political Officers, and detachments appear to have been pretty numerous. Moreover, on one occasion at least it played its part in what must have been a respectable encounter, when its services were called upon in connection with disturbances in the neighbouring state of Narsingh Garh. The Chief of this state, Rajah Chain Singh, had views of his own as to how his state should be governed, which did not quite accord with the views of the "Paramount Power." The British Government held that he had disposed of an uncongenial Minister by instigating his murder, and accordingly decreed Rajah Chain Singh's deposition. He was summoned to come into Sehore, and in complying with the summons answered that he accepted the invitation not only for himself, but for all his available armed forces as well.

On July 24th, 1824, this young Chief, with a following of some 400 fighting men, arrived at the outskirts of Sehore, near the junction of Siwan and Lotia Rivers, and was there attacked by a portion of the Bhopal Contingent and a small party of the 60th Native Infantry under the command of Captain De Waal. Chain Singh and 44 of his followers were killed and the survivors taken or dispersed. A memorial tomb marks the scene of this encounter close to where the road known as "Chota Chakker" joins the Indore road, the building being called "Chain Singh's Chattri," and is the object of considerable veneration.

During the 'thirties the Corps was commanded by Captain Winfield, who went on leave pending retirement in 1838. He seems to have acquired considerable popularity among the different ranks, for there is record of a movement being initiated to present him with a testimonial "in the form of some substantial present," which, however, was not permitted.

Second Reorganization, 1839. Cavalry, 256; Infantry, 516; with 30 of above Gunners.

Captain Winfield was succeeded by Captain Riddel. This officer's connection with the Corps was brief, but long enough, however, for him to draw up yet another scheme of reorganization, which was submitted to Brigadier-General Anquitel for criticism and report. The result of this report was the appointment of a second British officer, and the new organization provided for a muster of 256 cavalry, 516 infantry, with 30 sepoys of the latter trained as gunners. Captain J. E. Landers, from the 9th Native Infantry, was brought in as Commandant the following year—a coincidence, since the first number to be given to the Regiment proved in later years to be the IXth.

Third Reorganization.

Captain Landers commanded the Corps for a decade, and his time saw further changes. Possibly the experiment of substituting 30 infantry sepoys trained in gunnery for the original gunners had not been altogether successful, for the principal

A Bullock Battery formed.

Strength of the Contingent.

feature about the third reorganization was the introduction of 60 trained gunners (Golundaz), who formed a bullock battery of four guns. Besides these, the strength of the Contingent was fixed at a battalion of infantry of 600 men and 200 cavalry in four " Russalahs " or troops.

Although the days of the Pindaras were over, Central India was not without its troubles from dacoits and predatory tribes, and the Contingent found occupation not only in furnishing numerous detachments and escorts, but also in a good many minor punitive expeditions. In this way a serious encounter took place in 1845 with a body of " Wilayetees," as the records in the Political Agent's office at Bhopal term them. A good number of the said " Wilayetees " were slain, but during the course of the encounter the Contingent gunners were much hampered by the clumsy headdress they wore, which, judging by a description of this instrument of torture, is not to be wondered at.

Uniform in 1840.

The uniform of the Contingent infantry was a red tunic with black trousers, which, however, lacked the customary red welt down the outer seams of the legs. The Golundaz, or artillerymen, wore a blue tunic and a broad red stripe down the trousers, something after the pattern of dress worn by the Royal Regiment in early Victorian days. White pantaloons used to be taken into wear as the weather became warmer, and " white clothing " was worn by all ranks during the hottest months. The red and blue tunics, worn during the cold weather, had no facings, but the old-fashioned stiff " stock " was worn by everybody, embroidered with gold lace for British and Indian officers, pipe-clayed for the rank and file. Up to the year 1849 the headdress had been an enormous shakoe about eighteen inches high, fitting tight round the skull but splaying out to an unusual breadth at the top. It was surmounted by a red pom-pom, and was no doubt an imposing if inconvenient adornment. The shakoe itself was literally built of a bamboo scaffolding, covered with thick dark cloth, ornamented by a heavy brass badge and brass curb-chain, worn cross-wise and looped up on the right near the top of the edifice, which was secured to the wearer's head by a second curb-chain worn on the point of the chin. This abominable instrument of torture was considered in its day to compare favourably (!)—that is, to be more imposing, and no doubt heavier and more painful—with the headdresses worn by other Native regiments. It is necessary to suffer to be beautiful, but the contretemps which occurred when dealing with the "Wilayetees" in 1845 relegated the merely beautiful to a secondary consideration, and after considering the matter in all its aspects for another four years, cloth Kilmarnock caps, with a red ball of stuff on the top, and a small brass badge varying for the different companies, were substituted in 1849. The 1857 records mention "Wax-cloth covers" as being worn that year.

A further addition of British officers had been made, and, in 1847, Major Landers had serving under him Captain J. Travers as second-in-command, and Lieutenant Trevelion as Adjutant. Of these officers, and in fact of all who had hitherto done duty with the Contingent, Captain (subsequently General) James Travers is by far the best known in connection with the Regiment. Appointed early in the 'forties, he held the positions of Adjutant, Second-in-Command and Commandant successively, to which latter post he was appointed when Major Thomson, who had succeeded Major Landers, vacated in 1854 after four years' tenure of command.

James Travers, V.C., C.B., 1847 to 1860. Commandant 1854 to 1860. A Great Shikari.

Colonel James Travers is well known on many accounts. A gallant soldier, he was actually in command of the Contingent during the dark days of 1857, and, after the suppression of the revolt in Central India, was appointed the first Commandant in permanency of the newly-formed Bhopal Levy, or in other words, of the infantry regiment now existing. It is true that the raising of this Corps is attributed officially (*e.g.*, in the Quarterly Indian Army List) to Captain J. Peyton, but the latter was only officiating for Colonel Travers, duly appointed Commandant, during such time as Colonel Travers's other duties necessitated his absence from Sehore. As soon as he joined, Captain Peyton reverted elsewhere; and although this officer had actual charge of the preliminary work, there is no doubt that it was Travers' influence and Travers' name that brought the men to the ranks. His reputation as a shikari still lives among the oldest inhabitants of the Bhopal State, and used to be freely quoted to sportsmen in embryo a few years ago, much to the modern sportsman's disadvantage. Amongst other distinctions, he is credited with having killed over a hundred tigers within a twenty miles' radius of Sehore alone. Of recent years one had to go a little more than that to get one at all. A fund called the Travers Fund, for the relief of widows and orphans of men who belonged to the Regiment, was founded by him and further contributed to by Mrs. Travers after his death. This still perpetuates his name in the Regiment.

The officers serving under Colonel Travers were Captain F. L Magniac, Second-in-Command, and Lieutenant A. C. Lilly, Adjutant. The composition of the force had yet again been altered, though the date remains unrecorded, and stood at that time at 72 artillerymen, 255 cavalry and 712 infantry in eight companies. Further European supervision had been provided for by the appointment of warrant or non-commissioned officers (as was generally the case with Native regiments in those days), of whom mention is made of Sergeant-Major Enright, Staff-Sergeant Murphy and Sergeant-Major Bleazby. Probably each of these was concerned with one branch of the Contingent only.

Strength and Composition in 1857.

The British officers must have been unusually versatile, for they appear to have exercised command and to have been responsible for the training of the three arms quite indiscriminately, being one day cavalry, the next infantry, and the third artillery. Whether they were "specialists," or whether the specializing was left to the warrant or non-commissioned officers, is not recorded, but the following extract from the Contingent Order Book, dated March 28th, 1857, shows how things were worked :—

British officers. Their work.

"The following parades are ordered for the ensuing week at a quarter to 6 a.m. :—

"On Monday, the Cavalry.
"On Tuesday, the Infantry.
"On Thursday, the Artillery
"On Friday, the Cavalry.
"On Saturday the Infantry.
"On Wednesday at a quarter past 6 a.m., the whole of the force on the Infantry parade ground for muster."

It would seem from the above that, ordinarily speaking, two parades a week fell to the lot of each arm, but that sometimes, when the first of the month, or muster day, fell within the week, somebody might be so unfortunate as to have to undergo three. These parades are said to have lasted one hour exactly unless they were dismissed earlier. It would seem that the sepoys, sowars, or golundaz of those days could hardly complain of overwork, whatever the lot of their British officers may have been.

Recruiting Areas.

For a good many years past the rank and file had not been recruited locally; in fact, the experiment of doing so had, in the very early years of the Contingent's history, failed completely. About this time the Corps appears to have been generally representative of the fighting classes enlisted by the Bengal Army, the greatest number, counting the three branches of the force together, coming from Oudh and the neighbouring provinces. The Punjab, however, supplied its quota both to infantry and cavalry, and the latter was practically entirely composed of men from the land of the five rivers. Sikhs and Muhammadans, Rajputs and Brahmins in the eight companies of infantry were indiscriminately mingled, the guiding principle being, apparently, to have as nearly an equal proportion of each class in each company as possible. The men of the artillery are said to have been Brahmins and Muhammadans of Oudh only, which is a very interesting point when one comes to consider the behaviour of the Contingent generally during the year. Bullocks provided the traction power for guns, limbers and artillery waggons; the cavalry was on the Sillidar system.

CHAPTER II.

THE CONTINGENT IN 1857.

EARLY in this year there would appear to have been a somewhat restless spirit abroad in the Contingent. Courts-martial were of frequent occurrence—though the occasional interchange of the term "Court-martial" with "Panchayet" is confusing, and does not make it very clear as to how the said Courts were conducted or what powers they possessed. Insubordination to Native officers was the most common form of crime, but that any serious complications were entirely unanticipated is shown by the fact that Colonel Travers proceeded on leave early in the year. Captain F. L. Magniac was appointed to the temporary command during his absence, whilst Lieutenant A. C. Lilly doubled the duties of Second-in-Command and Adjutant. The usual escorts for the cold-weather tours of the Agent to the Governor-General in Central India and of the Political Agent in Bhopal had been furnished, and the usual reliefs to the detachments or "Outposts," as they were then called, were carried out. The most important of these "outposts" was at Indore—which was, and still is, the headquarters of the Central India Agency—and Bairaseea (the orthography is taken from an Order Book of the period), a place whose importance has entirely vanished since those days.

The first note of alarm is sounded in a Contingent Order of March 6th, wherein "the infantry and artillery guard against fire and thieves" was increased from 18 to 27 men. A special order of the same date forbids the singing of "ribald and indecent songs" in the lines or Bazaar during the "Hooly" by the men of the Contingent as, it somewhat naïvely adds, has sometimes occurred. On this date also the pay of the Corps seems to have miscarried somehow or other, as it was eventually advanced by the Political Agent "from his own resources."

Colonel Travers returned from leave on March 17th, possibly having been recalled owing to the circumstances of the time. The following extracts marked by inverted commas are taken from the old Contingent Order Book of that year. On March 27th a Subedar was deprived of the command of his company "as he has failed so conspicuously in carrying out orders which had been issued on more than one occasion." About the same time a havildar was ordered to rejoin Headquarters, "with a view to being brought to trial for disobedience of orders." On April 1st some 120 men of all ranks proceeded on leave till November 15th, and on the next date a large number of men were punished for living out of the lines contrary to orders. Another interesting record shows that the pay of the Contingent for the February was not disbursed until April 4th.

Shortly after this the cavalry guard against fire was increased to 12 men, and the whole 39, including the infantry-artillery mixed guard, were ordered to be "posted regularly and in uniform, the infantry with bayonets, the others with swords." Two more Courts-martial, one on a havildar, the other on a duffadar, were also recorded. On April 23rd the Contingent was paraded for the purpose of "hearing read the G.O.G.G. in Council of March 27th ordering that the 19th Regiment N.I. be disbanded for mutiny, and to hear the Court-martial, with remarks by H.E. the Commander-in-Chief, upon two sepoys of the 2nd Grenadiers." The first, of course, had reference to what are now historic events at Berhampur and Barrackpur, near Calcutta.

The present pages appear to have reference to what were little else than disciplinary Courts, but, truth to tell, records are scanty, and such as there are naturally refer to such matters which had to be published in the ordinary routine. At the risk of boring the patient reader, yet one more will be mentioned. On April 27th a Court-martial (five Native officers) tried Sowar Hirsa Singh, the sentence of which bears repetition if only as throwing some light on the terms of service in those bygone days. The Court sentenced the prisoner "to be transferred to the list of Bargheers, and his assameeship sold to Bargheer Hira Singh of the same troop. Order :—The prisoner will be released from confinement and return to his duty."

The meaning of this extraordinary sentence is made clear by an explanation of the system then prevailing. As in the ordinary Sillidar system in Indian cavalry in the twentieth century, the State did not provide horse, arms (except firearms), uniform or accoutrements to the cavalry-men of the Contingent. All these necessities had to be paid for by the soldier. A certain number of men were always ambitious of serving in a mounted corps who had not sufficient capital to pay for horse, uniform, etc., summed up in the comprehensive term, "their assami." On the other hand, many of the cavalrymen were persons of means, able not only to provide their own assami, but also that of some of their less wealthy comrades. These latter were called "Bargheers," or, in other words, hired men. The man who put the cash down was, of course, the owner of the horse, etc., and took the entire pay of the bargheer, giving him only some four or five rupees a month to subsist on. It thus followed that the bargheer was not so much the hired man of the Government he was supposed to serve as of the capitalist who felt inclined to invest his money in horseflesh and weapons.

Something very like hereditary service in the Contingent.

To such an extent was this system carried out in the Contingent cavalry that it was no uncommon thing for one man, actually serving in the ranks, to own as many as five or six horses ridden on parade by bargheers One naturally wonders what the general result of such a system could have been. One effect seems to have been the establishment of something very like hereditary service, for a Contingent Order of about the same time enlists one Pirtee Singh, "who is given the assameeship of the late Duffadar Tara Singh. *N.B.*—This assameeship is given in trust to Pirtee Singh until a son of Duffadar Tara Singh is old enough to be entrained. The monthly profits to be paid to the deceased's family."

Events at Indore cause Sir Henry Durand to move a strong detachment of the Contingent there.

Meanwhile, events had occurred in other parts of India. News from Meerut and Delhi had had its effect in Central India, and its reflex action is apparent in the Contingent Order Book. On May 16th a strong detachment of all arms, consisting of two companies of infantry, two troops cavalry and two guns, marched at "three or four hours' notice" towards Indore, "prepared to move on any special service required by Colonel Durand," who was then Agent to the Governor-General in Central India. Another company started in the same direction on June 7th, and an after order published the following day directs "the whole of the remaining cavalry and sufficient infantry to complete, with the detachment that marched the day before, two full companies to march this evening towards Indore." Two guns also accompanied this force, the whole being under the command of Colonel Travers. There is no record as to where they went, probably only as far as Ashta, for they returned to Sehore cantonment on the morning of the 16th and took over the treasury guard from the Durbar troops, who had undertaken this duty on the reduction of the Sehore garrison owing to the temporary absence of the above strong detachment. Courts-martial continued to be of frequent occurrence. There must have been a veritable glut of Medical Officers at that time, since no less than three are referred to in Contingent Orders during June alone :— Thus, " the guard over Dr. Trimmins' house is withdrawn," and " Assistant-Surgeon Thompson resumed medical charge of the Contingent, Assistant-Surgeon Westcott continuing to afford medical aid at Sehore."

Affairs at Indore continued to wear a threatening aspect, and in a few days' time yet another call was made on the Contingent. On June 12th a party, consisting of " 3 russaldars, 1 woordie-major, 2 jemadars, 2 kot-duffadars, 1 nisanchee (evidently our old friend the nishanburdar of 1824 under a slightly different name), 2 trumpeters, 35 sowars and 2 farriers proceeded forthwith towards Indore with the Commandant." Lieutenant A. C. Lilly was left in command at Sehore, where defensive measures were commenced, the Agency being prepared for that purpose. Colonel Travers and his party got through to Indore and joined a portion of the troops who had marched under Magniac on May 16th. Of Captain Magniac's original detachment, parties had been sent to Mehidpore and towards Sirdarpore.

Attack on the Residency at Indore.

An account of the oubtreak which occurred at Indore on July 1st is outside the scope of this work, as is also the attitude of the Maharajah Holkar and the State officials. These were matters of considerable controversy at the time, and subsequent voluminous writing on the subject has done little to silence such controversy. The Residency was attacked by the State troops and the populace. Colonel Travers had his horse shot under him, and two sowars of the Contingent were killed by the rebels. The road to Mhow, the nearest cantonment where a few British troops were stationed, was held to be impracticable, and the Residency position untenable. In these circumstances it was decided to evacuate Indore and to move eastwards to Sehore. This was done, the remainder of the detachment escorting the Residency officials and such other Europeans as had sought shelter there. The remaining 200 men of the Contingent, who had been left under Lieutenant A. Lilly, had been employed in putting the precincts of the Sehore Agency into a state of defence. It is recorded that a "stockade" was made, but the extent of the ground to be protected would rather point to the term being not altogether correct. Probably this position was partly stockaded, partly protected by walls and earthworks. Be that as it may, it was deemed impossible to maintain the post. Every other place in Central India had been lost already, the post was isolated and in the midst of a hostile population, and was, moreover, threatened by the regular Native troops at Saugor who had broken out into open mutiny; and so it was determined to abandon temporarily Sehore and to hold the line of the Nerbudda, which formed the boundary of British territory. A Contingent Order, dated July 9th, goes some way to explain the situation.

"An escort of cavalry and infantry of the Contingent, the former equal to 30 sowars with full complement of commissioned and non-commissioned officers, and the latter equal to 40 rank and file, composed of volunteers and only made up by roll if the volunteers do not equal the numbers above mentioned, will be held in readiness to escort the Political Agent and officers of the Contingent on their departure from Sehore."

Besides the Europeans usually resident at Sehore, there were also at that time a number of other people who had come for refuge from Indore, Agar and other stations. The Political Agent's office left for Hoshangabad on July 11th under the escort of 1 naik and 4 sepoys. The next day the Contingent officers and the remainder of the Europeans followed; the last Contingent Order—convening a "Native Court-martial" for the trial of certain sepoys who had not joined Headquarters with their company and who had lost their arms, was published immediately before departure. The cavalry of the escort accompanied them as far as the Nerbudda, and then disappeared. The infantry, 44 of all ranks, crossed the river and arrived at Hoshangabad and remained on duty the whole time. Of the other loyal

Last Contingent Order published July 12th, 1857.

remnant of the force, 227 infantrymen were drafted into the Shahgarh Military Police in January of the next year, whilst others joined the Sehore Military Police. The artillery as a complete body remained staunchly loyal and joined Sir Hugh Rose's force.

It is not easy to follow the why and wherefore of everything in the above narrative. Things might have been different, perhaps, had not certain political considerations intervened, but these considerations were held to be paramount, and so Sehore was abandoned. The Contingent cavalry, it is true, proved tainted, and badly tainted; but of the others there is a far brighter record. The conduct of the infantry escort to Hoshangabad, set forth in a dry matter-of-fact way, cannot well be weighed except by the consideration of happenings; and besides them, hundreds of the men remained loyal in the face of difficulties which the European mind can hardly estimate. A large number of these were drafted at the first opportunity into the various bodies of Military Police formed as Sir Hugh Rose's force advanced northward and eastward, whilst the artillery, as a complete unit, joined the same, and fought their guns at Jhansi under the command of Captain Fuller of the Bombay Artillery. Subsequently Lieutenant C. P. Roberts took over command of the Battery. The men of the Sehore Military Police, using the arms of the old Contingent, were placed at the disposal of the Political Agent as soon as he returned to that station.

And so " the old order changeth, giving place to the new." The days of the Contingent, that irregular mixed force raised originally to cope with the Pindaras, were over, and the time had come to substitute some other force to take its place.

CHAPTER III.

THE BHOPAL LEVY, 1859 TO 1865.

EARLY in 1859 the question arose of organizing a new permanent force to take the place of the old Contingent.

A purely Infantry Force. The Bhopal Levy, 1859.

After consideration as to whether this should or should not take the form of a new "mixed" force, it was decided to dissociate the idea of having mounted men and infantry in one and the same corps, and to raise a battalion of infantry, the nucleus of which was to be formed in Sehore (or Bhopal, for the two names were alternatively used). This, as has before been explained, consisted of men who had served in the Contingent infantry before the troubles of 1857. They had been collected at Sehore and armed, and were under the command of Captain W. Gordon-Cumming. On April 25th, 1859, Major A. L. McMillin took over temporary charge of this body of men from Gordon-Cumming. On this day also Lieutenant E. Temple was appointed Adjutant, whilst Assistant-Surgeon C. Thomson was nominated to medical charge.

These transactions form the substance of the first regular orders issued to the new force in the name of the Commanding Officer, and the Corps was henceforth styled "The Bhopal Levy," recruiting for which was opened from May 1st.

Colonel Travers was appointed Commandant, but being away from the station on other duty, he had no active part in the original formation of the Levy. His influence, however, effected a very great deal, and made the task of the officer selected to officiate for him an easier one than it would otherwise have been. This officer was Captain J. Peyton, of the 23rd Bombay Infantry, who relieved Major McMillin on June 10th, and proceeded forthwith with organizing and disciplining the new Corps. The permanent appointment of Second-in-Command was conferred upon Lieutenant R. C. Cross, who joined from the 17th Bengal Infantry; Lieutenant Temple, the Adjutant, has been mentioned previously.

Composition.

A large number of men from the Shahgarh Military Police Battalion (which also had been formed of men from the Bhopal Contingent infantry) were entertained, whilst other faithful men from the defunct

Gwalior and Mehidpore Contingents were also received. By June 1st the Regiment was divided into ten companies of some 40 men each, numbered from one to eight, while the flank companies were known as the "Grenadier" and "Light" companies respectively.

Subedar-Major Karam Sher Khan.

Promotions were made among the Native ranks to commissioned and non-commissioned grades, such men being selected as had distinguished themselves for loyalty and activity during the recent disorders. Among these promotions it is interesting to notice the name of Karam Sher Khan, who was appointed Pay-Havildar. This soldier had enlisted in the Contingent infantry in 1847, and formed one of the escort to Hoshangabad. Whilst there he attracted early attention for his zeal and staunch fidelity, and was selected for special employment. Carrying despatches backwards and forwards during the latter part of 1857, a duty which he performed with exemplary resource and courage, he managed to penetrate time and time again into Sehore and succeeded in conveying valuable official records and likewise property of Europeans to a place of safety. On one occasion when so doing, he was wounded and taken prisoner by a party of mutineers, who intended to hang him the following morning. Owing, however, to the lack of vigilance on the part of the guard set over him and to the assistance of a friend, he managed to effect his escape.

Karam Sher Khan continued to serve for many years after the reorganization of the Regiment, and subsequently rose to the rank of Subedar-Major, receiving the Order of British India. After his retirement he continued to live at Sehore and to take the greatest interest in the Regiment and its doings, always appearing as a spectator at any ceremonial parade of unusual interest, where his keen, intelligent face, white beard and perfectly turned-out uniform, old only in fashion, and accompanied by snow-white gloves, which were always worn by Sirdars in *his* day, formed quite a feature of the proceedings. He lived to see his old Corps delocalized, and accompanied the last party which marched out of Sehore, heavy at heart at the uprooting of so many ties. He died in 1908 at the age of eighty-three in the station where he had so long resided, but he had lived to see his relative of two generations later, Subedar-Major Shekh Ali Mahommed, occupy the same position of honour and responsibility which he himself had held.

Another interesting personality who joined about this time was Durgh Singh, who succeeded Karam Sher Khan as Subedar-Major. Like the former, he also provided one of a younger generation for the highest post in the Indian ranks of the Corps in the person of his son, Subedar-Major Ishwari Singh, who retired from that position in 1908.

The men of the Contingent Battery, which had served as an Artillery unit during the Central India Campaign, transferred to the Bhopal Levy, May, 1860.

In March of the following year (1860), Colonel Travers joined his appointment and Captain Peyton reverted to his former regiment. A further addition to the strength of the Corps was made by the transfer *en bloc* of the men of the old Contingent artillery. This battery had returned after the work of the Central India Field Force had been accomplished, and, though it had been decided not to maintain it any longer as an artillery unit, it was too good a body of men and its services had been too conspicuously loyal to ignore. The non-commissioned officers and men were therefore transferred to the Levy under the orders of the Agent to the Governor-General with effect from May 1st.

Detachments found by the Levy.

The Levy was split up into a large number of detachments, these being necessitated by the existence of surviving bands of mutineers and rebels who had taken refuge in the jungles of Central India. Tantia Topi had crossed and recrossed this tract of country, pursued and harried by the various mounted irregular corps, whilst the infantry were required to maintain various posts at likely places of vantage to him and his followers. The most important of these " Outposts," as they were called, were at Bairseea, Basoda, Bhilsa, Narsingh Garh, and Manora. To furnish all these detachments and to provide the numerous escorts, the actual strength of the Corps had to be brought up to establishment as rapidly as possible. With a view to bringing up the numbers quickly, the standard of height had to be reduced from 5 ft. 7 in. (which, with this temporary exception, has always been maintained for men in the ranks) to 5 ft. 3 in. The weapons with which the men were armed were those which had belonged to the Contingent, and many complaints as to their state and quality were made.

It was not intended to continue the old red uniform in the new Levy, but as yet no definite settlement had been made as to what should be substituted for it. For the time being the men were clothed in khaki drill. The authorities do not seem to have quite got over the fondness for cumbersome head-dress, for once more the bamboo scaffolding was built upon the sepoys' heads, but this time it was bound round with khaki puggri cloth. The weapons, about which complaints had been rife, were replaced by newer and more serviceable arms. An officers' mess was likewise properly established, but the Government allowance for the upkeep of the same was not sanctioned for another five years.

The Question of Uniform.

The European officers seem to have been subject about this time to a great deal of transfer between the Levy and the various bodies of irregular horse raised about the same time. Before the month of May was over, Colonel Forbes had succeeded Colonel Travers, the latter being permanently transferred to the command of "Meade's Horse." This latter corps was, with a number of other similar bodies, subsequently merged into the Central India Horse. Later on in the same year, Colonel Forbes also went, his place being taken by Captain E. W. Dun, who officiated in command of the Levy on two occasions. The transfer of Colonel Forbes (or Hamilton Forbes, as he was usually called) was only a temporary measure, and he remained permanent Commandant of the Regiment for nineteen years.

Colonel James Travers leaves the Regiment, 1860.

Colonel Hamilton Forbes.

The somewhat hasty manner in which the Corps had been brought up to strength made a certain amount of weeding out desirable in 1861. A number of men were discharged under a Medical Board, but a large number of Brahmins, who had enlisted under false castes, were more summarily dealt with. Orders had been issued originally to enlist this class somewhat sparingly, and in order to become enrolled a number of these men had passed themselves off as Rajputs. The deception having been discovered, nearly 150 of them were summarily discharged, their places being taken by the immediate transfer of 144 men from the Bhopawar Levy. Later on in the year some of the numerous detachments were withdrawn, as

Men of the Bhopawar Levy transferred to the Corps, 1861.

matters had resumed a more normal aspect. The enterprising Tantia Topi had been laid by the heels, and the usual cold-weather tours of the Agent to the Governor-General and the Political Agent were resumed. Escorts were provided, for the former a full company, for the latter a jemadar's party. A force of two full companies under a British officer proceeded on " special duty "—probably dacoit hunting, since small bands of these pests gave frequent occasion for the activity of small parties for the next thirty years and more. More sensible ideas of dress seem to have occurred to the authorities, for the first mention of " turbans" being worn is recorded during this year. The number of men on guard duty each day at Sehore was 126, and the list of detachments furnished was as follows (the orthography is that used in a letter of that date, and has a somewhat " Dundreary " flavour about it) :—

" Baiseeah.
" Bhilsa.
" Basodah.
" Narsinghar.
" Oojein.
" Chandgarh.
" Sirdarpore
" Burwanee, south of the Nerbudda."

The above formed the duties of the Bhopal Levy, and so continued until the Corps was brought under the provisions of G.G.O. 279 and 280 of 1864 regarding good conduct pay and scale of pay to Native officers. But the time had come for yet another change of name. Purely an infantry Corps, it was felt that the term " Levy " was not sufficiently descriptive. The Bhil Corps, the Central India Horse, the Deoli Irregular Force, or the Erinpura Irregular Force, all corps under the Government of India, explained lucidly by name alone what each was, and the " Levies " should therefore own a title which would do the like

CHAPTER IV.

THE BHOPAL BATTALION, 1865 TO 1903.

THE Corps was so designated under G.G.O. March 21st, 1865. The Native ranks of the establishment consisted of

10 Subedars (including one Subedar-Major).
10 Jemadars (including one Jemadar-Adjutant).
50 Havildars.
50 Naiks.
20 Drummers.
800 Sepoys.

The recruiting areas were Oudh, the Punjab, the North-West Frontier Provinces, Bundelkhand and the districts of Rohtak and Kangra; the above establishment remained undisturbed till 1903. This year also saw the introduction of the drab uniform for full-dress, with chocolate facings, and gold lace for the commissioned ranks. Blue puggris were worn by the Native ranks, and also blue puttees and Punjabi shoes. The red sash was worn by Native officers and non-commissioned officers, and the coat was of the "Zouave" pattern, the broad chocolate facing running down as far as the waist-belt. The tunic for British officers was cut in the same fashion as the ordinary infantry tunic, the sword belt worn outside, but instead of a sash a pouch belt was worn over the left shoulder. When mounted in review order, white buckskin breeches and Napoleon boots completed the costume.

The Uniform definitely decided on, 1865.

Drab: Chocolate Facings, Gold Lace. Unchanged till 1895, when Gold Lace Disappeared.

The Grenadier and Light Companies disappeared, the companies being numbered 1 to 10, the different classes of men enlisted being mingled in each. As far as possible, Sikhs, Brahmins, Rajputs and Muhammadans were equally enlisted, whilst Dogras and Hindus, other than the above, were entertained in a minor degree.

The Battalion's Lines.

A short description of the Battalion lines may be of some interest. The Native officers each owned their bungalows, purchasing the same when promoted from the person whose place they took. Apart from the family lines, which accommodated rather more than the authorized proportion, the bachelor lines

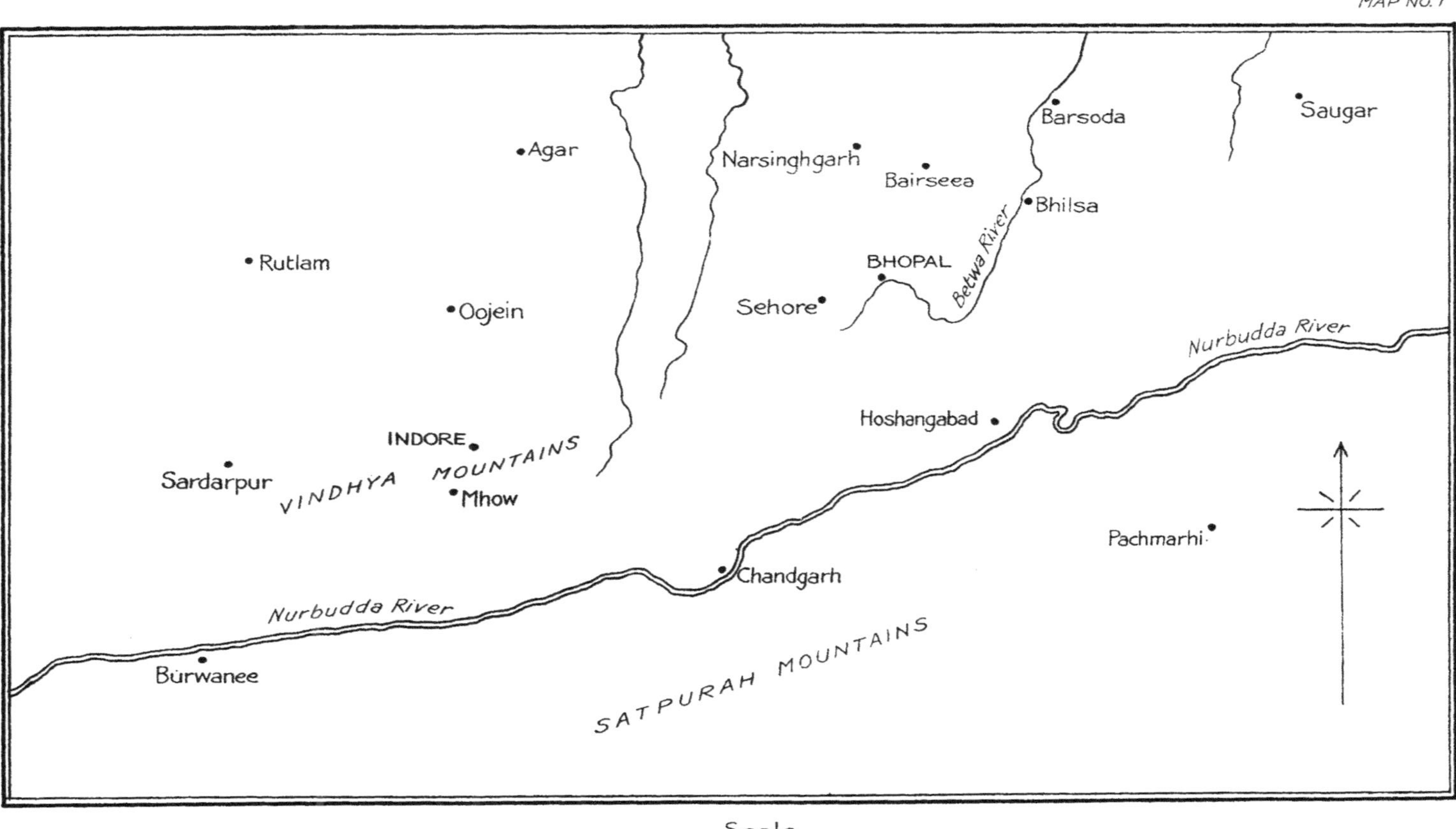
MAP OF CENTRAL INDIA
MAP NO. I
Agar
Narsinghgarh
Bairseea
Barsoda
Saugar
Bhilsa
Rutlam
BHOPAL
Betwa River
Sehore
Oojein
Nurbudda River
Hoshangabad
INDORE
VINDHYA MOUNTAINS
Sardarpur
Mhow
Pachmarhi
Chandgarh
Nurbudda River
SATPURAH MOUNTAINS
Burwanee
Scale
Miles 40 30 20 10 0 40 80 120 160 Miles

also consisted of separate small rooms for each man. This plan, of course, prevented the carrying out of a proper "barrack" system, but it was very much appreciated by the men and worked well enough under old conditions. Wood for construction and repair was obtained free from the Bhopal jungles, shady trees were everywhere, and water was generally plentiful and good.

Minor operations were carried out in the Satpura Hills during 1865, but the records of this time were not written up very completely, and nothing more can be said about them.

An officer joined the Corps in 1868 who was destined to have a longer connection with the Corps than any other so far. This was Lieutenant G. R. Peart, who came on transfer from the Central India Horse. Going through all the various stages of rank, and holding in turn every appointment open to him, he relinquished command in 1895 on attaining fifty-five years of age. Another officer of the old school who joined two years later was Captain C. Ransford; remaining twenty-four years with the Regiment, he retired as Lieutenant-Colonel in 1894.

British Officers.

A fourth British officer was authorized about 1873, in which year a Regimental School was established. Most of the outlying detachments had been withdrawn, but Indore was now regularly furnished with a full company. This was from time to time temporarily increased as occasion required, and three companies went there in 1875, under the command of Captain Ransford, for the reception of the Viceroy. In February, 1876, the Headquarters of the Regiment, under Colonel Forbes, were present at that station on the occasion of the visit of H.R.H. the Prince of Wales.

On the outbreak of the Afghan War, in 1878, the Regiment, leaving a small depot at Sehore, proceeded in November on service to the North-West Frontier. Till this time the Battalion had been armed with muzzle-loading rifles (the Enfield), but these were exchanged for breech-loading Sniders. The officers accompanying the Corps were :—Colonel Hamilton Forbes, Captain G. R. Peart, Lieutenant E. S. Masters, Lieutenant W. J. Orr and Surgeon J. L. Corbett.

Afghan War, 1878-79.

The Battalion held part of the line of communications

from Jamrud to Dakka during the first phase of the war, and was in the division of General Maude. In April, 1879, Colonel Forbes was appointed to the command of a brigade in the Kurram Valley Field Force, Colonel H. M. Wemyss assuming command of the Battalion for the time being.

The terms under which the corps under the Government of India were serving were none too clearly defined at that time, and an authoritative announcement was necessary on this point. This was contained in Letter No. 1399 H.C., dated March 11th, 1879, under which the Regiment was amenable to the Indian Articles of War whilst serving in the field or when brigaded with other troops of the Indian Army. The Battalion returned to Sehore on July 9th, 1879.

Afghan medals were received by the Regiment from H.E. Sir Donald Stewart, G.C.B., Commander-in-Chief in India, at Bhopal on December 15th, 1882. Major G. R. Peart was temporarily in command, officiating for Lieutenant-Colonel J. D. Hall, who had been brought in from the Central India Horse on Colonel Hamilton Forbes leaving the Regiment

Addressing the Battalion, the Commander-in-Chief said :—

Sir Donald Stewart addresses the Regiment, 1882.

" From my own observation I can say that it is as fine a Regiment as I have seen in this country; and its steadiness on parade and general appearance do great credit to yourself [Major Peart] and the officers of the Regiment."

Major Peart was the senior officer remaining with the Regiment who had accompanied it on service. The Regiment, under G.G.O. of 1881, was entitled to bear the distinction " Afghanistan, 1878-79 " on its appointments.

Establishment of the Band.

Soon after the return from Afghanistan a band was established, and Ghaffur Khan was the first Band Havildar. He was soon after made Bandmaster, and was subsequently promoted to Jemadar. After being pensioned, his services were still retained until about 1907, when he relinquished his position after nearly a quarter of a century's charge. All ranks originally contributed to the support of the band, and the customary allowance of Rs100 a month was sanctioned from the outset. British officers' subscriptions stood for many years at one half per cent. of their pay and allowances.

The Regiment was not actively employed during the

second phase of the Afghan War (1880), but a wing under Captain Ransford marched to Agar to relieve the Central India Horse, and remained there till the following year, when it rejoined Headquarters.

Rifle Shooting and Re-arming.

A rifle club, for the purpose of improving the shooting of the Regiment, supported entirely by regimental subscription, was established in 1883, with excellent results. In addition to winning outright the Rajputana and Central India Challenge Cup—a handsome trophy obtained by the then secretary of the meeting, Captain O'Moore Creagh, V.C., who subsequently became Commander-in-Chief in India—the Regiment had the distinction of being placed first in order of merit among all corps armed with the Snider rifle. In recognition of this fact, an early opportunity was taken to re-arm the Battalion with the Martini-Henry rifle, considerably before its turn would have come round in the ordinary course of events ; the Bhopal Battalion was therefore the first of the local corps to be armed with a long-range, effective breech-loader.

Lieutenant-Colonel Hall relinquished the command in 1885 and was succeeded by Lieutenant-Colonel J. Miller, who was brought in from one of the other corps under the Government of India. His tenure was a very short one, and he retired the following year.

Regimental Colours.

Since the reorganization of the Regiment, Colours had not been carried. But in the old Contingent days, in addition to the cavalry guidons already mentioned, the infantry also bore Colours. The former were taken into the Officers' Mess, where they have been hung since 1893, but of the latter there is no trace beyond the fact that they were for a long time kept in the Quartermaster's Stores. Their disappearance coincided with the retirement of Lieutenant-Colonel Miller.

Lieutenant-Colonel G. R. Peart was the next Commandant, remaining so for a period of nine years, and had serving under him Major C. Ransford, Second-in-Command, Captain E. S. Masters, Adjutant, also Major Jasper Burn, Lieutenants Watson, H. L. Goodenough and C. C. Levison-Gower. Surgeon A. H. C. Dane was Medical Officer of the Regiment and also in collateral medical charge of the Bhopal Political Agency. This arrangement continued until 1897, when it was turned the other way about, the Agency surgeon holding collateral medical charge of the Regiment. Arthur Dane's connection with the Regiment lasted from 1881 to 1902.

From 1886 to 1888 the usual detachment of one company at Indore was increased to three companies under a British officer. The Headquarters of the Regiment, under Lieutenant-Colonel Miller, also marched there to take part in the reception of H.E. The Viceroy, Lord Dufferin.

In 1887 the different classes intermingled in every company in the Regiment were sorted out and Caste Companies were formed as under :—

Formation of Class Companies, 1887.

"A" Company :		Sikhs.
"B"	,,	Sikhs.
"C"	,,	Hindustani Muhammadans (Sheikhs, Sayeds, Pathans).
"D"	,,	Brahmins.
"E"	,,	Rajputs.
"F"	,,	Dogras.
"G"	,,	Mixed Hindus (mostly Ahirs).
"H"	,,	Brahmins.
"I"	,,	Rajputs.
"K"	,,	Muhammadan Rajputs (Rangars, as they were then called).

There is little to note during the next few years. The Regiment, under Colonel Peart, marched into Bhopal on the occasion of the visit of H.E. The Viceroy, Lord Lansdowne, and was inspected on another occasion by H.E. the Commander-in-Chief, Lord Roberts. Captain Masters took up the appointment of Cantonment Magistrate, Secunderabad, and was succeeded as Adjutant by Lieutenant J. H. Pollard. Lieutenant Dennis Peart, a son of the Commandant, joined in 1891, as did Lieutenant F. C. L. Waller the same year, neither of them having any long connection with the Corps. Lieutenant C. B. Baldock joined in 1892, and Lieutenants C. B. Thornhill at the end of the previous year.

Action against the Mogias.

About this time a detachment of about half a company was furnished at Nowgong.

In 1893 extensive operations were undertaken by the Thaggi and Dacoity Department for the suppression of that class of crime, and certain Mogias, coming under unfavourable notoriety in that respect, had to be rounded up by parties of the Regiment. One of these parties under Jemadar Chede Khan, succeeded in capturing a considerable number of one of these gangs after a bit of a scuffle, in which some of the Mogias were killed.

Colonel Peart proceeded on leave to England, and the officiating command of the Corps devolved upon Lieutenant-Colonel C. Ransford. Captain G. G. J. Sutton Jones was brought in from the Deoli Irregular Force to act as Second-in-Command, and Lieutenant C. C. Jackson also joined. The former officer did not remain long with the Regiment on that occasion, as urgent affairs necessitated his taking leave about four months after he joined, but he was destined to return a few years later as permanent Commandant.

The reason why so many officers passed through the Regiment about this time—there were others besides those mentioned—was because the local corps in Central India and Rajputana were regarded as forming a group of units for the purposes of promotion and appointment. Moreover, the question of leave was dealt with in an extremely liberal spirit, and every time an officer went on leave, or even took up an officiating extra regimental appointment, even of the most temporary nature, some other officer arrived to complete the quota of four combatant officers plus a doctor.

The Regiment in those days was inspected annually by the General Officer Commanding at Mhow. Railway communication between Mhow and Sehore was not very convenient, as the journey necessitated, firstly, crossing the Nerbudda River, always an unpopular proceeding, a change of gauge at Khandwa, and, lastly, a long drive by road. However, the high-road between Mhow and Sehore was, though long, of a good quality and afforded easy access to several " jhils " with excellent shooting. Hence the journey by the road proved the most popular, in spite of the fact that it took a very long time to inspect the Bhopal Battalion.

Lieutenant-Colonel Ransford left the Regiment in 1894, being succeeded as Second-in-Command by Major E. S. Masters, who likewise followed Colonel Peart as Commandant the next year. Colonel Peart's departure was made the occasion of a great send-off, each man in the Regiment giving him an individual farewell as he passed through the lines for the last time. Lieutenants S. R. Davidson and

G. V. Holmes joined the Corps in 1894 and 1895 respectively, Lieutenant C. C. Jackson succeeded Captain Pollard as Adjutant, and Captain C. Hutton Dawson was brought in as Second-in-Command.

Havildar Badhawa Singh.

Opportunities for sport were not lacking. The Regiment had a happy hunting-ground peculiarly its own at Lotia, and the surrounding jungles at Khajuri and Lawakheri were visited year by year. Colonel Travers' fame as a shikari has already been mentioned. A good many of the men became very expert in marking down tigers and running a beat, of whom Rur Singh, Choharja Singh and Havildar Badhawa Singh were best known and in most request. The last named, a Nai Sikh, was a particularly fine fellow, endowed with magnificent nerve and coolness. On one occasion (1896) a tiger had been wounded and turned back on the beaters, who were under the command of Badhawa Singh. The beaters took to the trees, small saplings, covered by Badhawa Singh with an old Martini-Henry carbine and six rounds of ammunition. The tiger's wounds prevented it moving very fast, and Badhawa Singh fired all six rounds at it as it came on straight at him, and then swarmed up the last available stem, the brute striking at him and covering his dhoti with blood and foam. The officers managed to get to the spot and dispatch the tiger before further harm was done, but it was then found that *every one of Badhawa Singh's six shots had reached its mark.* A few days later this non-commissioned officer was in a train which caught fire, going at full pace. The doors were locked and everybody perished except Badhawa Singh, who rolled himself in his bedding and somersaulted through the window.

The last of Government of India Charge.

Major Masters died of cholera in 1896, and was succeeded by Lieutenant-Colonel G. A. Collins. The Battalion underwent a very searching inspection by H.E. the Commander-in-Chief, Sir George White, in November, who devoted several days to it, especially with regard to field work. Lieutenant E. T. Carwithen joined during the year. The following year the Bhopal Battalion was placed under the orders of the Commander-in-Chief in India with effect from February 15th, and the station of Sehore was incorporated in the Nerbudda District of the Bengal Command. Its direct connection with the Government of India, by whom all appointments and promotions had been made, was severed after a period of sixty-nine years.

During 1897 Major Hutton Dawson, Lieutenants C. C. Jackson and S. R. Davidson left the Regiment. Major A. Poingdestre, Lieutenants H. L. Anderson and F. W. Thomas joined. Captain Pollard had exchanged somewhat previously with Captain B. P. S. Rooke of the Scinde Horse. Lieutenant-Colonel G. G. J. Sutton Jones obtained the command in 1899, Captain Rooke becoming Second-in-Command and Captain H. L. Anderson Adjutant. The two Indian officers who successively obtained the rank of Subedar-Major about this time were Raghubar Pershad Tiwari, a Brahmin, and Buta Singh, a Sikh.

Lieutenant-Colonel Sutton Jones, a keen soldier and an indefatigable shikari, was all too short a time with the Regiment. Operated on for liver abscess, he failed to rally from the shock, and died at Indore in the autumn of 1900. Lieutenant-Colonel G. H. J. Moore was brought in to succeed him, and Lieutenant T. E. M. Lane joined.

Recruitment of Jats.

More recent changes had included the idea of improving the personnel of the mixed Hindu Company by introducing Hoshiarpore Jats into it, and some two sections of men of this class were enrolled in it. An addition was also made to the strength of the British officers. But all these minor changes were swamped in a general reorganization of the Regiment in 1903. The .303 in. magazine rifle had been issued the previous year, and the time had come to further assimilate the Regiment to the conditions governing other northern regiments of the Indian Army

CHAPTER V.

THE 9TH BHOPAL INFANTRY, 1903 TO 1904.

Finally re-organized as a Regular Regiment, 1903.

IN 1903 the Regiment, under a scheme for a redistribution of the numerical titles of all corps in the Native Army, was re-named the 9th Bhopal Infantry. The Dogra and the mixed Hindu Companies were eliminated and an addition of 20 men was made to each of the remaining companies. These eight companies were then brought together by classes into four double companies as under :—

Class Composition.

" A," " B," " C," " E " and " H " Companies remained as before.
" K " Company (Muhammadan Rajputs) became " D."
" D " Company (Brahmins) became " G."
" I " Company (Rajputs) became " F."

The original " F " (Dogras) and " G " (Mixed Hindus) disappeared. Thus the composition of the Regiment was equalized as to its classes of men enlisted.

" A " and " B " formed No. 1 Double Company—Jat Sikhs.
" C " and " D " formed No. 2 Double Company—original Muhammadans and Muhammadan Rajputs.
" E " and " F " formed No. 3 Double Company—Rajputs.
" G " and " H " formed No. 4 Double Company—Brahmins.

The following officers were appointed to the Regiment: Lieutenants W. K. Rollo, R. W. Gaskell and 2nd-Lieutenant G. D. Martin; and shortly afterwards Lieutenant L. J. Jones and Major Henry Comins, the latter as Second-in-Command.

The establishment remained the same as regards the number of sepoys, but the change entailed a reduction of 2 subedars, 2 jemadars, 10 havildars and 10 naiks. But on the other hand advantage was gained by the admission of all Native ranks to the full privileges of pay and pension of the Indian Army.

The list of officers under whom these changes had been effected was as follows :—

Commandant : Lieut.-Colonel G. H. J. Moore.
No. 1 Double Company Commander : Captain H. L. Anderson.
No. 2 Double Company Commander : Captain T. E. M. Lane.
No. 3 Double Company Commander : Captain C. C. Jackson.
No. 4 Double Company Commander : Major Henry Comins.
Lieutenant L. J. Jones, who was appointed Adjutant.
Lieutenant W. K. Rollo.
Lieutenant R. W. Gaskell.
Second-Lieutenant G. D. Martin.
Subedar-Major Ishwari Singh.

Major B. P. S. Rooke and Captain E. T. Carwithen were seconded from the Regiment at the time, the former never rejoining. Lieutenant-Colonel P. A. Weir (I.M.S.) was in collateral medical charge.

Delocalized, 1904.

In the following year (1904) the Regiment was delocalized and placed in the table of reliefs to go to Allahabad, their place at Sehore being taken by the 46th Punjabis. The foregoing sketch of the history of the Regiment was compiled during the course of this year by Captain C. C. Jackson, and the information was obtained partly from old regimental records (which, however, were of a somewhat scanty nature), partly from records in the office of the Political Agent, Bhopal, by the kind permission of Major J. Manners Smith, V.C., and partly from the office of the Agent to the Governor-General in Central India. Intimate friendship with various old pensioners, and likewise with certain British officers of a bygone generation served to elaborate somewhat the dry matter of fact detail culled from official sources, and explained various points which would otherwise have remained obscure. This friendship did much to make the task an entirely congenial one.

The Headquarters of the Regiment marched out of Sehore on November 7th, 1904, leaving a detachment behind pending the arrival of the incoming regiment. Major

Henry Comins was in actual command of the Corps at the time of the exodus. The last party remained till the end of January 1905, when it, too, proceeded to Allahabad under Captain C. C. Jackson. Thus a tradition of nearly eighty-seven years was broken, and the quiet little station in Central India had ceased to be the permanent residence of the Regiment which had been so long identified with the State of Bhopal and its ruling house.

CHAPTER VI.

1904-1914.

THE Regiment marched via Saugor, where it was rejoined by its Commandant, Lieutenant-Colonel G. H. J. Moore, from leave on November 18th, arriving at its new destination on December 17th, 1904.

Full establishment of British Officers appointed.

After leaving Sehore and during the early part of 1905, several new officers joined the Regiment, among whom were Lieutenant W. A. T. Ferris, 2nd-Lieutenant R. E. Harenc, Major C. F. Dobbie, 2nd-Lieutenant F. V. Pogson, 2nd-Lieutenant A. R. O. Mallock and Lieutenant H. H. Smith. In February, 1906, the Signallers of the Regiment were congratulated by the General Officer Commanding the 8th (Lucknow) Division, on the high figure of merit they obtained.

In May, 1906, owing to several new appointments, the establishment of British officers was brought up to twelve for the first time. The officers with the Regiment at this time were :—

Commandant : Major C. A. Brown.
1st Double Company Commander : Major C. F. Dobbie.
2nd Double Company Commander : Captain E. T. Carwithen.
3rd Double Company Commander : Captain T. E. M. Lane.
4th Double Company Commander : Lieutenant H. H. Smith.
Adjutant : Lieutenant L. J. Jones.
Quartermaster : Lieutenant G. D. Martin.
Lieutenant G. B. C. Irvine.
Lieutenant C. G. Ransford.
Lieutenant W. A. T. Ferris.
Second-Lieutenant F. V. Pogson.
Second-Lieutenant A. R. O. Mallock.

On December 12th, 1906, the Regiment marched to Agra, arriving there on January 10th, 1907. On January 12th the Regiment took part in the Grand Review before the Amir, leaving the following morning and reaching Allahabad again on February 9th, 1907.

The first mention of a Camp of Exercise appears to be made when a strength of 10 British officers, 13 Native officers and 574 rank and file were at Shiurajpur from November 4th to the 26th, 1907.

Nothing of importance is recorded until, on December 16th, 1908, the Regiment left Allahabad by rail for Burma with Major C. F. Dobbie Commanding. At Calcutta the Regiment embarked on the R.I.M.S. *Harding*, arriving at Rangoon on December 22nd, where they relieved the 72nd Punjabis. A detachment of 2 British officers, 5 Native officers and 290 rank and file were sent to Port Blair in the Andaman Isles. The Port Blair detachment was relieved by the 93rd Burma Infantry and returned to Headquarters, Rangoon, on January 24th, 1910.

Service in Rangoon.

On September 22nd, 1910, Colonel C. A. Brown issued his farewell order and was relieved by Major C. F. Dobbie. On March 24th, 1911, the Regiment embarked on the R.I.M.S. *Northbrooke*, landed at Bombay on the 31st and arrived at Fyzabad on April 3rd, where it relieved the 11th Rajputs. On May 11th, 1911, the Regiment was issued with the magazine Lee-Enfield Mark II rifle, which was again changed on June 12th, 1913, to the Short Mark III .303 rifle. From January 15th to 28th, 1914, the Regiment took part in the Lucknow Brigade manœuvres.

Re-armed.

PART II.

SERVICE IN FRANCE: 1914-15.

CHAPTER VII.

EARLY MEASURES.

On the outbreak of war, the 9th Bhopal Infantry was stationed at Fyzabad, where it had already spent three and a half years. Fyzabad was in every way an excellent station. All arms of the service were represented in the cantonment; all ground around affording every facility for tactical exercises, hence training was carried on under almost ideal conditions. It was a cheery place, sport was good, and all the time the Battalion was there every one was happy. It was not a mobilization station, orders therefore to mobilize early in August, 1914, came as a very pleasant surprise.

Service in Fyzabad.

The Battalion was then organized in eight companies, composed of one double company of Sikhs, one of Muhammadans from the United Provinces and Southern Punjab, one of Rajputs from the United Provinces and one of Brahmins.

Before the war most battalions had " links," but there were a few exceptions, and the 9th Bhopal Infantry was one. The " link " system was bad enough and had many disadvantages, but a battalion with no " link " was greatly handicapped when reinforcements were sent to it.

Indian Army Organization.

The war proved that the Indian Army organization was at fault. When reinforcements were received they came from many units who differed, not only in class and speech, but even in training, hence officers and men knew nothing of each other. It also proved, as previous wars had done, that the human factor is as important as ever. It is not sufficient to collect a crowd together and to think that they can fight; the spirit may be there, but cohesion and co-operation will be lacking. When reinforcements are received they should be acquainted with the unit and know something of its ways; in fact, they must be imbued with a regimental spirit. The present training battalion system, where the recruits of all battalions in a group are trained together in one common school, is the result of one of the lessons learnt during the war. It is not intended, when making the above remarks, to belittle the magnificent and, at times, superhuman efforts and sacrifices which the Battalion made in 1914, but to show that the Indian Army was not organized to carry on a war on a large scale.

Arrival of Mobilization Orders.

The news of a war came as a great surprise to the quiet station of Fyzabad, where the hot weather was proceeding very much as usual with a number of officers and men on leave. Suddenly this station was roused by mobilization orders for the 9th Bhopal Infantry on August 9th, at 10.30 a.m. All British officers of the Battalion on leave in India were at once wired to return, and orders for the recall of the men were issued. But the Regiment was too quick for the post office. August 9th was a Sunday, the clerk who took the orders to the post office soon returned with all the envelopes and with a note from the postmaster saying that no action was possible as it was a Sunday. The despatch of the mobilization orders had therefore to wait till the following day.

Mobilization.

In those days, the stores of field service clothing were kept by the Supply and Transport Department; these stores were at once issued to the Battalion. The ensuing days were very busy ones. On August 12th three men reported their arrival, next day 76 men, and so on. There was a good deal of delay in the post office in sending the mobilization papers to the soldiers, some of whom never received them, but turned up on hearing the proclamation of mobilization. On August 14th Army Headquarters wired, ordering the Battalion to leave for Karachi at 6.45 p.m. on August 15th. As yet a large number of the men on leave and reservists had not returned, so, to complete the numbers up to field service strength, the Battalion was ordered to draw upon the 17th Infantry at Lucknow for its Muhammadans and the 89th Punjabis (now 1st Bn. 8th Punjab Regiment) at Dinapore for its Sikhs, Rajputs, and Brahmins. As many as 52 non-commissioned officers and men were required from the 17th Infantry and 111 non-commissioned officers and men from the 89th Punjabis. It may be mentioned here that neither of these two battalions had any connection with the 9th Bhopal Infantry; the kits of the drafts differed from each other and the 9th Bhopal Infantry, but the two regiments sent their best men and they did splendidly on service.

At 4 p.m. on August 15th the Battalion fell in, and marched down to the station amidst great enthusiasm from masses of people who had come up from the city and neighbouring villages; the entraining took place at 5 p.m., and by 6.30 p.m. the Regiment was ready to start. During the hot weather a battalion is often short of some of its British officers absent on leave. On this occasion Lieutenant-Colonel H. L. Anderson, Second-in-Command, Captain R. W. Gaskell, Captain H. Etlenger, Captain E. V. Wills and Lieutenant R. D. S. Banks, the Quartermaster, were on leave in England. Captain N. H. H. Ralston, Adjutant, recently operated on for appendicitis, and Lieutenant A. V. Myles were on the sick list. The following officers were with the Battalion when it left Fyzabad :—Lieutenant-Colonel C. F. Dobbie, Captains G. Jamieson, Jones, Irvine, Martin (officiating Adjutant), Lieutenants Mullaly, Wade and Browning. The Medical Officer was Lieutenant Brock (I.M.S.). On the fifth day the train reached Karachi, the Battalion detraining at 10 a.m. on August 19th and camping at the rest camp.

Departure from Fyzabad.

On arrival at Karachi, the 9th Bhopal Infantry came under the orders of the Ferozepore Brigade (Brigadier-General R. C. Egerton commanding, with Captain Sangster and Captain Stewart as Brigade Major and Staff Captain). The few days at Karachi were spent completing the Indian mobilization arrangements, issue of three months' pay, etc. The Brigade Commander inspected the Battalion on August 21st. While at Karachi a number of men rejoined, being sent on from the depot at Fyzabad, thus causing a surplus owing to the men that had been taken on from the 17th Infantry and 89th Punjabis. This surplus had to be returned to their units, and eventually only 37 men were taken on from the 17th Infantry and 1 Indian officer and 64 men with two followers from the 89th Punjabis. The Battalion was now to proceed overseas in two ships, half a battalion on the ss. *Ellenga* and half on the ss. *Teesta*. Troops were ready to embark but the ships were not ready. On August 24th half a battalion, consisting of Nos. 2 and 3 Double Companies, embarked on the ss. *Ellenga* with the 129th Baluchis, who also belonged to the Ferozepore Brigade.

Arrangements at Karachi.

Colonel Nawab Nasurullah Khan of Bhopal, Honorary

Colonel in the Battalion, wired for permission from the Government of India to accompany his unit on service. This permission was given. He joined the Battalion at Karachi and embarked on the ss. *Ellenga*. Colonel Nasurullah Khan had not been in the best of health, but he was keen to do his duty in the war and was determined to accompany his Battalion on service. Unfortunately, on board ship between Karachi and Aden, he was taken seriously ill ; the medical officers would not allow him to proceed any further than Aden, from which place he had to return to India and never really recovered his health. The Battalion deeply regretted Colonel Nasurullah Khan's departure, and wish to record their appreciation of his keen sense of duty and loyalty. He had always been a very good friend to the Battalion, popular with all ranks, and he continued to be so until the day of his death.

Colonel Nawab Nasurullah Khan.

On August 25th orders were received to embark the rest of the Battalion on the ss. *Teesta,* together with the 57th Wilde's Rifles. Although the troops were embarked, there was considerable delay before the ship left Karachi ; this was no doubt due to the hurried way ships had been collected and converted into transports. Aden was not reached till September 7th, the ss. *Teesta* forming one of the convoy of seven ships escorted by the R.I.M.S. *Northbrooke.* The destination of the troops had been kept secret until Aden was reached, when it appeared in " Reuters " that Lord Kitchener had made a statement in the House of Lords that two Indian divisions were on their way to France.

On September 13th Suez was reached, and everyone was surprised when orders were issued to disembark and proceed by rail to Cairo. There was some delay before the disembarkation took place, the Battalion not reaching Heliopolis till the evening of the 15th. The reason for the move to Cairo was not very apparent, as, by the evening of the 17th, fresh orders were received to re-embark on the same ships at Alexandria. While at Cairo, the Indian organization of a battalion was dropped and the Home organization adopted. The word " double " company was no longer used, the old double company being known as a company, and this company divided into four platoons. The new drill had to be explained and taught as quickly as possible ; it was not

Service in Egypt.

very easily grasped by the men, whose minds were already being filled with the new scenes. The British officers who had been on leave in England rejoined here. On the 17th the Battalion moved to Alexandria. But the orders for immediate embarkation were somewhat premature, as the ships had not reached Alexandria and embarkation could not therefore take place till the 19th, the convoy sailing at midday. Two days out from Alexandria a large convoy of outward-bound ships, conveying a complete territorial division for India, was met. The sight of a large number of vessels meeting in mid ocean was very impressive, especially to the Indian soldier, and gave him some idea of what is meant by sea-power.

Arrival at Marseilles.

At last, on September 26th, very early in the morning the first convoy of transports from India reached Marseilles; at 9 a.m. disembarkation commenced and proceeded without a hitch. The news of the arrival of Indian troops soon spread through the city, and dense crowds came down to view these strange troops who were coming to the aid of France. All the way from the quay to the camp at Parc Borelli the enthusiasm of the crowds was genuine and intense; no Indian troops have ever had a warmer reception, and they thoroughly appreciated the welcome from the French. Lieutenant-Colonel J. W. B. Merewether and the Right Honourable Sir F. Smith's book entitled, "The Indian Corps in France," thus describes the welcome :—

"On marching away from the docks to their camping-ground, the troops met with a remarkable reception. Our warm-hearted allies, men, women and children, vied with each other in showing honour and kindness to the men who had traversed so many weary miles by land and sea to play their part in the World War at its most critical period."

Preparations in Marseilles.

At Parc Borelli the two half-battalions were again united. Here the 9th Bhopal Infantry found itself as a unit in the Ferozepore Brigade, the other battalions consisting of the Connaught Rangers, 57th Wilde's Rifles and the 129th Baluchis. The Ferozepore Brigade was part of the Lahore Division, commanded by Lieutenant-General H. B. Watkis, C.B., whose brigades were called the Ferozepore, Jullundur and Sirhind; the latter was detained for special reasons in Egypt, and did not rejoin the division for some weeks.

As soon as units reached Marseilles they were re-armed with a new rifle and ammunition; this was unavoidable, the reason being that units from England were using Mark VII ammunition, the only kind now being manufactured. Warm underclothing also had to be issued; all this took time, and it was not until September 30th that battalions were ready to move north. On September 29th a divisional route march took place through Marseilles which was witnessed by thousands of cheering inhabitants. On September 30th the Battalion left Marseilles and detrained at Orleans at 1 p.m. on October 2nd. The camp was at Champs de Cercottes, some four miles away, where the Lahore Division was being concentrated and issued with transport. The train journey from Marseilles was remarkable for the warm reception given to the Indian troops at every halting place, large crowds collecting at each station, where the train stopped, offering gifts of cigarettes, milk, fruit and sweets to the men.

Orleans.

The Lahore Division, less the Sirhind Brigade, remained in this camp till October 16th. The time was fully taken up with company, battalion and brigade training, varied with route marches and inspections. On October 5th General Sir James Willcocks, who had been selected for the command of the Indian Corps, inspected the Ferozepore Brigade. On October 8th Prince Arthur of Connaught inspected the Battalion. At this camp home pattern transport was issued; the G.S. wagon, however, was not available, its place being taken by civil carts of all descriptions and sizes. General Sir James Willcocks, in his book entitled, "With the Indians in France," gives a very graphic account of this heterogeneous transport:—

"A vast plain, now converted into a bog, was literally strewn with vehicles and horses; every species of conveyance found a place, and the fair at Nijni-Novgorod could not have shown greater variety; the charabanc and the baker's cart; structures on prehistoric springs; pole and draught horses; horses in hundreds without collars, head or heel ropes, in fact just loose. It might have appeared grave if it had not been so amusing. But the cart horses and harness were all as nothing to the drivers. Good fellows, who a month later had become useful soldiers, to-day they were indeed a sore trial. . . . The Indian soldiers could not understand all these things."

At Orleans the battalion left behind its first "reinforcements" and entrained on October 17th for the battle area.

Condition of the Indian Troops.

Let us pause for a moment to consider the Indian soldiers. They had travelled far; thousands of miles of land and sea separated them from their homes. Their minds were full of strange scenes that were being enacted around them; they saw a strange people friendly and civilized, but who spoke a language which they could not understand and, what was more, they were entering a strange war, the like of which they had never for a moment contemplated. The danger to India did not seem to worry them; the "Sirkar" had gone to war, they had eaten the "Sirkar's" salt for years, and now it was their duty to go wheresoever they were sent. This traditional loyalty was founded deep. It was due in a very great measure to their British officers, whom they regarded with esteem and a genuine affection. These officers had trained them from boyhood, both in soldiery and games; they knew them better than anyone else, these men would now lead them to victory. They never paused to think what would happen when these British officers should fall, as they did from the very beginning. When this happened for a time they were worried, but, to their credit be it said, they never lost their pluck or their loyalty. When posterity reads the record of the doings of the Indian troops in France, it must be grateful and give full credit to these Indian troops for a self-sacrificing spirit and for the part they took in those critical days while the Empire was preparing.

Whilst at Orleans, His Majesty the King-Emperor graciously sent the following message to the Indian troops in France:—

"Officers, non-commissioned officers and men, I look to all My Indian soldiers to uphold the 'izzat' of the British Raj against an aggressive and relentless enemy. I know with what readiness My brave and loyal Indian soldiers are prepared to fulfil the sacred trust on the field of battle, shoulder to shoulder with their comrades from all parts of the Empire.

"Rest assured that you will always be in My thoughts and prayers.

"I bid you go forward to add fresh lustre to the glorious achievements and noble tradition of courage and chivalry of My Indian Army, whose honour and fame are in your hands."

CHAPTER VIII.

THE BATTLE OF NEUVE CHAPELLE, OCTOBER, 1914.

(See map facing page 48.)

Various Billets.

On October 18th the Battalion detrained at Wizernes at 1.30 p.m. and moved directly into billets. This was the first occasion in which the Indian troops were billeted; two companies were located in a brewery and two in a girls' school. On October 21st at 12 noon the Ferozepore Brigade marched out via Saint Omar-Arques towards Bailleul. The night of October 21st-22nd was spent in bivouac and part in some farms, the march being continued at 6.25 a.m. on the morning of the 22nd. As the Brigade marched, a number of buses were sent back from the front to pick up battalions and take them forward quickly; in this way the Connaught Rangers, 57th Wilde's Rifles and 129th Baluchis were embussed during the day and hurried forward to the support of General Allenby's Cavalry Corps. The 9th Bhopal Infantry marched escorting the transport of the three units. The night of the 22nd was spent in billets just north of Bailleul. At 5.45 a.m. on the 23rd, the Battalion continued its march via Neuve Englise and Kemmel to Voormezeele, which place was reached by 3 p.m. where it billeted.

The General Situation.

It will now be necessary to give a very brief account of the general situation. The Cavalry Corps were holding the ground from Zandvoorde to Wytschaete. Between these places the ground rises in a ridge several hundred feet high, and the occupation of this ridge by the enemy would have compelled the evacuation of Ypres The fighting that ensued was very severe. On October 21st the Germans had commenced their great effort to capture Ypres and drive the heavily outnumbered British forces into the sea. The Connaught Rangers were attached to the 1st Cavalry Division, the 57th Wilde's Rifles and the 129th Baluchis were with the 2nd Cavalry Division. The 9th Bhopal Infantry was kept in "Corps reserve" at Voormezeele. On October 24th the Battalion was moved forward to the fifth kilometre stone on the St. Eloi road to act as reserve to the 2nd Cavalry Division, which was being attacked; later in the evening it was withdrawn to Voormezeele. On the 25th orders were received for the Battalion to move up and occupy the trenches held by the 57th Rifles.

Move to Vielle Chapelle.

On the 26th the Battalion had actually fallen in at 8.30 a.m. with a view to moving up to these trenches, when fresh orders were received directing the 9th Bhopal Infantry to proceed by bus at once to Vielle Chapelle, where it was reported that the Germans had broken through. The buses did not arrive till 5 p.m., at which hour the Battalion embussed and started for Vielle Chapelle. Travelling all night, the Battalion reached its destination at 7 a.m. on October 27th and prepared some food. At 11 a.m. it was ordered to move to Rouge-Croix to take part in an attack on Neuve Chapelle. The situation in this area was very critical. The enemy had gained a considerable local success, driving a salient into the sector of the British line held by the 7th and 9th British Brigades. At 5 p.m. a message was received that the Germans were pouring through Neuve Chapelle, that the Wiltshires and South Lancashires were nearly surrounded and had been forced to give up a good deal of ground. It was evident that a gap had occurred between the 3rd and 5th British Divisions, and it was necessary to counter-attack at once. By the time the orders to counter-attack had been issued it was getting dark, and there was little time to reconnoitre the ground, which was by no means easy; the situation, too, was very obscure. In addition to this, the Battalion was without its machine guns which were being employed near Ypres in support of the 57th Rifles. These guns, under the command of Captain Gaskell, did not rejoin the Battalion for some days. Lieutenant Browning also was away commanding the Brigade small arm ammunition column near Voormezeele.

Private description of the Battle.

The following abbreviated account has been taken from the diary of Lieutenant-Colonel C. F. Dobbie, who was in command of the Battalion at that time:—

"I was ordered to take command of an attack which was now developing on Neuve Chapelle, the troops involved were part of the Royal Scots Fusiliers, 600 French Chasseurs, half battalion 47th Sikhs and the 9th Bhopal Infantry. The Royal Scots Fusiliers and French Chasseurs formed the firing line, the 47th Sikhs in support and the 9th Bhopal Infantry in reserve. Touch between these units was very soon lost. The 9th Bhopal Infantry moved to the actual attack at about 4.45 p.m. just as it was getting dusk; Nos. 2 and 3 Companies were in front, and Nos. 1 and 4 in support. The situation was very obscure, and heavy rifle fire was heard in front. Lieutenant-Colonel Anderson, wishing to find out the situation sent out a couple of men under Lieutenant Mullaly. Unfortunately, before Lieutenant Mullaly had gone very far, he was captured by a strong party of Germans, whom, in the increasing darkness he had taken to be British troops.

"The country over which the Battalion was advancing was extremely difficult, and made more so by dykes, hedges, barbed wire fencing and darkness. No previous reconnaissance had taken place, nor was this possible; companies began to open out in trying to find a way through the obstacles; No. 2 Company, under Captain Jamieson, inclined to the right; No. 3 Company, under Lieutenant-Colonel Anderson, was hindered temporarily by some difficult fencing which surrounded an orchard. Meanwhile, I was with a platoon of Sikhs from No. 1 Company, when we suddenly bumped a party of Germans whom we partially surrounded I tried to get them to surrender, but, as another platoon of Sikhs was coming up on our left the enemy bolted, though not before a number of casualties had been inflicted on them. We re-formed the Company and reached the Royal West Kents' headquarters. Eventually the whole Battalion assembled there.

"After a short consultation with the Officer Commanding the Royal West Kents, I detailed companies off to hold various portions of trenches. It was 8 p.m. before we were settled down. I now learnt that Lieutenant-Colonel Anderson was severely wounded and Lieutenant Mullaly was missing. No sooner had we entered the shallow trenches than the enemy delivered an attack on us, which was easily repulsed

"Soon after midnight another attack was made, the brunt of which fell on No. 1 Company; this, too, was repelled with heavy loss to the enemy.

"When the situation had quietened down, I took stock of things, and ordered forward our left companies so as to conform with the general line. Considering the darkness and the complete ignorance of the ground, this was very well done, and we gained some 200 yards with very little loss.

We then re-dug ourselves in the new line. At about 4 a.m. the enemy attacked once more, using searchlights, Vérey lights and illuminating bombs. This attack was pressed till about 6 a.m. without being able to move us from the shallow trenches.

"We sadly needed barbed wire, but there was none. At about 9 a.m. the G.O.C. 7th Infantry Brigade determined to clear the village of Neuve Chapelle, and sent for me. By the time I got back it was 11 a.m. and the attack was to start at 11.15 a.m. after a short bombardment. I hadn't time to collect the Company Commanders, and therefore sent the Adjutant off to tell them verbally to co-operate as soon as the guns ceased firing. The 47th Sikhs were on the left, between them and us came two companies of Sappers and Miners, who had been brought up during the night to fill the gap between us and the 47th Sikhs ; on our right were the remnants of the Royal West Kents.

"Considering the hasty arrangements that had been made, the men gained a good deal of ground to start with, and some actually reached the original line from which the Wiltshires had been driven out the previous day. The enemy then launched a strong counter-attack, preceded and well supported with a heavy bombardment. I saw Jones wounded ; I heard Wade was killed and then Irvine wounded. In face of the appalling fire the men held on splendidly, but the enemy came on line after line, and by sheer weight of numbers drove us back. The withdrawal started on the left, No. 1 Company was the last to be driven in, although it had lost all its officers. Martin, seeing the men going, ran across a fire-swept beetroot field, rallied them and took them forward again. These held on and did splendidly. Later the line was swept back again. I, with Havildar Amar Singh (afterwards Subedar, and awarded an I.D.S.M.), and a few men went back and held on to a piece of trench. The shelling was very severe ; as the cover was inadequate, the men had no protection. A platoon of No. 3 Company, with Captain Wills, did splendidly, hanging on to their portions of trench for several hours until they were withdrawn under orders. At 9 p.m. the remnants of the Regiment collected near Pont Logy."

The official diary of the Battalion gives an account of this fight. The Officer Commanding 9th Bhopal Infantry was given verbal orders to move forward and assist the

Royal West Kents and carry them forward into their trenches, which they were to occupy The Battalion moved forward from Rouge-Croix with its right on the main La Bassée Road. In darkness and enclosed country, bogs and barbed wire fences, cohesion was lost, but eventually the whole Battalion reached the Royal West Kents' trenches, which had never been vacated by then. Companies commenced entrenching at once, but it was found that the left of the West Kents was in the air, hence fresh dispositions were made. The situation was critical. The enemy had practically enveloped the left of the West Kents and were actually firing into them from the rear. The 9th Bhopal Infantry, arriving on the right flank of these Germans, forced them to retire and so protected the left of the Royal West Kents. As soon as positions were occupied the men entrenched, the only tools available being the small Sirhind tool which the men carried on their equipment. Patrols watched the front up to Neuve Chapelle. A report was made by a machine gunner of the Royal West Kents that Lieutenant-Colonel Anderson, who was inspecting his dispositions, was lying wounded in a lane and his orderly killed near him; also that about thirty Germans were holding the gardens bordering the lane. A conference between a staff officer, Officer Commanding 9th Bhopal Infantry and Officer Commanding Royal West Kents resulted in bringing up two companies of Sappers and Miners on the left of the 9th Bhopal Infantry to fill up the gap. Frequent attacks were made by the enemy during the night, a searchlight played on the left all night; several snipers remained behind the line, causing a number of casualties. At about 11 a.m. a bombardment of our guns commenced and lasted fifteen minutes. Written orders were now received for an attack to be made by troops facing Neuve Chapelle. The attack was not co-ordinated, units advancing independently.

Account of the Battle in the War Diary.

The original trenches from which the Wiltshires had been driven out the previous evening were reached. The enemy then started a severe bombardment on this thin line, and supported it with a strong counter-attack, which drove in our left and then gradually forced the rest of the line to give way. In the withdrawal, unsupported by fire, the Battalion suffered many casualties, and eventually the remnants of the Battalion collected on the road south of Rouge-Croix. On the right Captain Wills, with a platoon of No. 3 Company, maintained his position till 2 a.m., although the enemy had driven in the supports of the Royal West Kents and had occupied ground in rear.

Casualties.

The casualties were heavy and amounted to :—6 British officers, 5 Indian officers and 262 rank and file. Of the British officers, Lieutenant-Colonel H. L. Anderson, Captain L. J. Jones and Lieutenant Wade were killed ; Captain G. B. C. Irvine wounded and Lieutenant J. C. D. Mullaly missing and Lieutenant-Colonel C. F. Dobbie sick.

Among the Indian officers, Subedar Pertab Singh and Jemadar Sidh Nath Misr were killed and the rest wounded. It will be seen that the Battalion lost heavily in British officers. Lieutenant-Colonel H. L. Anderson had joined the Battalion as a subaltern, a most efficient soldier, who was habitually looking to the comfort of his men as well as to their training, and was loved by them ; he would have succeeded to the command of the Battalion and his loss was a very severe one. Captain Jones was a splendid type of regimental officer, absolutely fearless, good at all games and respected by all ranks. Lieutenant Wade had joined the Battalion only about twelve months before ; a gallant officer, a young life full of promise was abruptly ended ; the men felt his loss very much as he always took a keen interest in them. Lieutenant-Colonel C. F. Dobbie was a sick man before he left India, but was determined not to give up on the Battalion being ordered on active service, and equally determined to command it in action ; the strain was beyond his physical capabilities, and he never recovered from this action. His was a very severe loss, as he continually had the interests of officers and men at heart. He had been with the Battalion for nine years, and the Battalion missed him very much. Captain G. A. Jamieson assumed command of the Battalion.

Frequent Moves.

On October 29th the Battalion moved to Estaires, where the men found some food awaiting them ; they had now been without a meal since the 26th. The same afternoon the Battalion moved out to Pont Dohem, arriving there at 10 p.m. On November 1st it was ordered to Rue de Paradis. During these exciting days it was employed as a reserve and frequently transferred from one brigade to another ; on one day it had four such transfers.

It was well known that the Germans were making a great effort to break through on this front; the German Emperor was reported to have arrived and to be conducting the operations in person. The General Officer Commanding-in-Chief the Indian Corps, Sir James Willcocks, called upon all ranks to repeat their magnificent efforts. On November 3rd the Battalion was occupying trenches near Rue de Paradis. A heavy bombardment on the Manchesters took place that night, but no attack materialized.

Rue de Paradis.

On the night of November 4th/5th the Battalion took over trenches from the Royal Scots Fusiliers. These trenches were held till November 8th. During this period no serious attack was made, but the Battalion was subjected to severe bombardments which caused a number of casualties. On November 7th, at about 4.30 p.m., in under ten minutes 55 men were killed and wounded. At 11 p.m. another heavy bombardment took place resulting in fifteen casualties, the total casualties on the 7th and 8th amounted to 1 Indian officer (Subedar-Major Bhure Singh) and 75 other ranks. The Subedar-Major's loss was a severe one; he was a most gallant officer, and was commanding his company after Lieutenant-Colonel H. L. Anderson became a casualty. He had been awarded the I.D.S.M. for his gallantry on October 28th. He recovered from his wounds and worked in the Depot until the end of the war.

At 10 p.m. on November 8th the Battalion was relieved by the Connaught Rangers, and moved to Rouge-Croix. On the 9th orders had been received to move to Estaires, and the Battalion was actually on the march there when ordered back, as an enemy's attack was expected. On the 10th it reached Estaires, where it was seen by General Sir J. Willcocks, who congratulated the men on their fight of the 28th.

The story that has been told above describes the part which the 9th Bhopal Infantry took in the immense battle which had commenced on October 21st and which continued without a lull until the end of the first week in November. This was one of the most critical periods in the war. Sir John French thus acknowledges the efforts of the troops in this great battle :—

" No more arduous task has ever been assigned to British soldiers, and in all their splendid history there is no instance

BATTLE OF NEUVE CHAPELLE

27TH. and 28TH October, 1914.

British line at 6 a.m. 28TH. Oct.

MAP NO.2

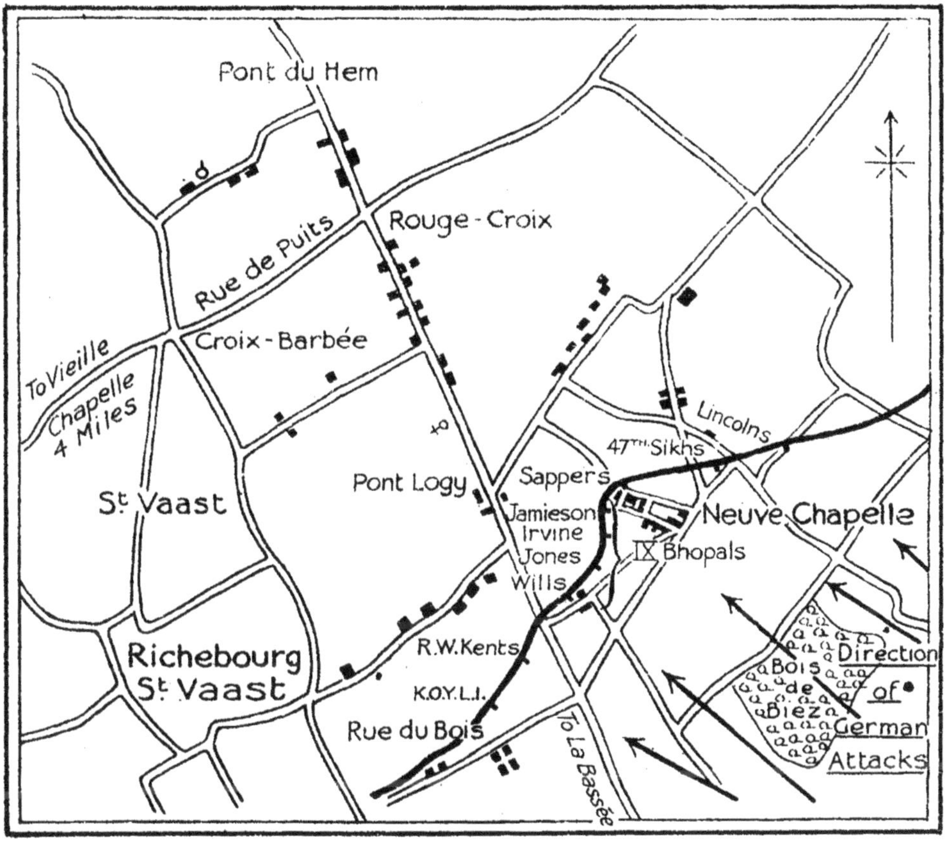

Pont du Hem
Rouge-Croix
Rue de Puits
Croix-Barbée
To Vieille Chapelle 4 Miles
St. Vaast
Pont Logy
Lincolns
47TH. Sikhs
Sappers
Jamieson
Irvine
Jones
Wills
Neuve Chapelle
IX Bhopals
Richebourg St. Vaast
R.W. Kents
K.O.Y.L.I.
Rue du Bois
To La Bassée
Bois de Biez
Direction of German Attacks

Scale

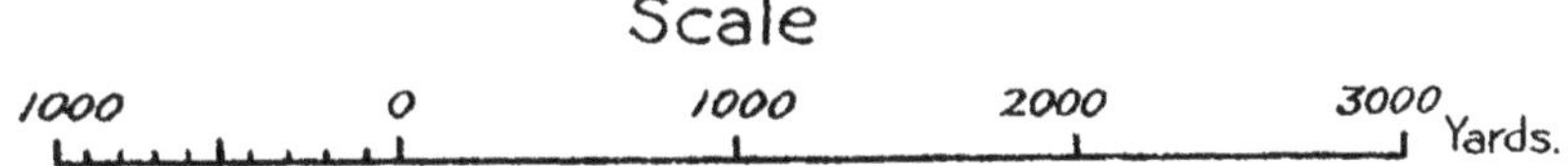

of their having answered so magnificently to the desperate calls, which of necessity were made upon them."

On November 12th Field-Marshal Earl Roberts saw and spoke to selected men of the Indian contingent in the market square at Estaires. He caught a chill at this inspection and died two days later.

On November 12th the first reinforcement in officers arrived in the Battalion, Major H. C. Carleton, 90th Punjabis, and Captain Apthorpe, 90th Punjabis, joining the Battalion. Major Carleton assumed command and held the command for the next eight months He had a most difficult task; the Battalion owes him a debt of gratitude for the way in which he fulfilled his arduous duties. He was unknown to a single officer or man; he had to take over a battalion sadly depleted and inevitably shaken, and restore them as a fighting machine.

Arrival of Reinforcements.

On November 16th, Lieutenant G. Balfour, 98th Infantry, joined, and on the 17th Lieutenant Fletcher, 97th Infantry, and Captain Mortimer, 10th Jats, joined. There was little opportunity given to rest and re-form, for between November 17th and 22nd the Battalion moved from Estaires to Beaupre and then to Les Lobes. On the 21st one company had the honour of being inspected by H.R.H. The Prince of Wales. The weather had now turned very cold indeed, snow falling on that day. The men and officers were still wearing their Indian pattern khaki drill, for no warm uniform had as yet been issued.

CHAPTER IX.

FESTUBERT, NOVEMBER, 1914.

(See map facing page 70.)

ON November 22nd at 10 a.m. orders were received that the Ferozepore Brigade was to relieve the Bareilly Brigade that evening, and that the 9th Bhopal Infantry were to take over the trenches now held by the 2/8th Gurkhas and 6th Jats, near Festubert. The relief was carried out as soon as it was dark, and completed by 10 p.m., Nos. 3 and 4 Companies, under Captains Gaskell and Mortimer and Lieutenant Fletcher occupying the fire trenches, and Nos. 1 and 2 Companies, under Captains Apthorpe and Wills, the support trenches. Lieutenant Balfour commanded the machine guns. The first line transport, under Lieutenant Banks, moved to Goore. The 59th Rifles, Frontier Force, were holding the trenches on the right of the Battalion and the 34th Sikh Pioneers the trenches on the left.

The night of November 22nd-23rd was a particularly quiet one, and nothing of importance occurred till 8 a.m. on November 23rd, when gradually the sound of bombs bursting in the trenches of the 34th Sikh Pioneers was heard. The noise became louder and louder, and news then filtered through that enemy bombers had forced their way into these trenches. The bombing attack was serious, as the 34th Sikh Pioneers had no means of coping with it. It had become possible as the enemy had gradually sapped up to our trenches, the leading sap being within five yards of the front parapet when the Brigade took over the line. It was unfortunate for us that the enemy had selected the 23rd for their attack, as the troops were new to their trenches and so did not know them.

German Attack on November 23rd.

It soon became apparent that this local bombing attack was developing into something bigger and more serious. It became necessary to send up both of the supporting companies of the 9th Bhopal Infantry to assist the 34th Sikh Pioneers. The Battalion thus lost its own supports. At 11 a.m. it was clear that the 34th Sikh Pioneers were unable to hold their trenches. The bombing attack now began to affect the left flank of the 9th Bhopal Infantry At

11.30 a.m. Captain Gaskell reported that the enemy were in possession of the trenches on his left, and that he was very anxious about that flank. He therefore asked that the supports might be sent up and protect this flank, but this was impossible, as the supporting companies were now occupying the support trenches on which the 34th Pioneers were falling back. Soon after this telephone communication with the fire trench broke down. A runner was sent up to try and get a message to Captain Gaskell, but returned with the information that the enemy was now between the fire trench and Battalion Headquarters. Gradually the Germans surrounded Nos. 3 and 4 Companies, who were putting up a stout fight against heavy odds. The fighting became hand to hand; our men were handicapped by having no proper bombs to keep the enemy at a distance. Between 2.30 p.m. and 3 p.m. it became obvious that these two companies had been overrun. The General Officer Commanding Ferozepore Brigade now arrived at Battalion Headquarters The 2nd/8th Gurkhas and 6th Jats had been brought back, and they counter-attacked as soon as they arrived, but were unable to recover the lost ground. Meanwhile, several other units had been brought up and further counter-attacks launched without any real progress being made, until the arrival of the 1/39th Garhwal Rifles and 2nd Leicesters. These two battalions organized a bombing counter-attack, one coming from the left and one from the right, and eventually regained the lost trenches.

The casualties in the Indian corps in endeavouring to recover the ground had been very severe, for the fighting had been very largely hand to hand.

The gallant way in which the 9th Bhopal Infantry tried to stem the advance of the enemy down their trenches was shown by the number of bayonet wounds which the men received. An officer of the 1/3rd Gurkhas found the body of Jemadar Mulloo Singh lying over a dead enemy whom he had strangled. Jemadar Mulloo Singh was a great loss. He was the Jemadar Adjutant, and had volunteered the previous night to go back to his old company as it was short of Indian officers. Subedar Faiz Ali Khan's body was found pierced with several bayonet wounds. He was a fine type of Indian officer, truly respected and beloved by his men. Just before the counter-attack took place he was heard encouraging his men, saying, " To-day is the day to show what we are made of. I will lead you and will be the first to die."

Altogether the Battalion lost over 200 men in this fight Again the loss in British officers was heavy. Captain Mortimer, 10th Jats, was killed; he had only joined six days before; he was an officer with much experience, and his loss was keenly felt at this time. Captain Apthorpe was severely wounded; he, too, had only recently joined and could ill be spared. The Battalion had a sad loss in Captain Gaskell. At first it was feared that he had been killed, but later it was known he was a prisoner. Lieutenant Fletcher, who had only joined a few days before, was also captured.

Casualties.

Among the Indian officers, Subedars Faiz Ali Khan, Baijnath Singh and Jemadars Mushtaq Ali and Mulloo Singh were amongst the killed, while Jemadar Ramsurat Missir was missing. It will be seen that the losses in officers were very severe, and the Regiment, already heavily depleted, could ill afford these.

The Indian Corps lost more than 40 British officers on November 23rd in recapturing these 1,000 yards of trenches.

After the fight the remnants of the Battalion were withdrawn into the reserve trenches. They were employed in holding them by day, and used for work on improving communication trenches by night. On the night of December 3rd the Battalion moved to Croix de Fer. It remained here till the 13th, being employed in digging rearward lines. On the 6th General Sir J. Willcocks came to see the men and the latest reinforcements which had been sent from India. These consisted of 4 Indian officers and 180 men. A word must be said here regarding these reinforcements.

As the Depot in India belonging to the Battalion was unable to supply its needs, it became necessary to call upon other units of similar composition for reinforcements. These were at first sent indiscriminately without their Indian officers and non-commissioned officers. When posted to the Battalion in the field, the men did not know their comrades or their commanders. Fighting efficiency consequently suffered. This mistake was realized later, and complete sub-units such as platoons or troops under their own Indian officers were sent. In this instance the men were drawn from the 1st Brahmins, 21st Punjabis, 96th Infantry and our own

Reinforcements.

Depot. Major Carleton had not sufficient men for a full battalion, and he organized the Battalion into two companies, one of Sikhs and Rajputs, the other of Muhammadans and Brahmins. On December 8th Captain C. H. Jardine, 96th Infantry, and Lieutenant Taylor, 1st Brahmins, joined the Battalion. Captain Jardine was an officer with a great deal of war experience, having fought in the Matabele and the South African Wars. Captain Dempster and Lieutenant Fasken joined on the 10th. At this time there were only two British officers left of the original Battalion.

On December 12th the Battalion had its first official bath at Béthune, hot water baths being supplied, and men's clothing changed at the same time. The little insects which affectionately attached themselves to officers and men not only caused annoyance, but also brought on a "lice fever." These baths were greatly appreciated, and later were supplied frequently when out of the trenches. On the 14th the Battalion moved to Gorre, where it was joined by Captain Cavendish, 97th Infantry. On the 16th orders were received to move up to the trenches near Givenchy. The Battalion was now about to take part in its third great battle.

CHAPTER X

GIVENCHY.

FROM about the middle of December the Indian Corps had been carrying out a series of local attacks, " with a view to containing the enemy now in their front," in order to assist the II Corps under General Smith-Dorrien, then attacking near Messines.

General Situation.

On December 16th the Ferozepore Brigade delivered an attack, the 142nd French Territorial Battalion taking the place of the 9th Bhopal Infantry, who were being rested for a few days. On the 18th the Indian Corps was to demonstrate along the whole front ; the Ferozepore Brigade was in position just east of Givenchy, and the Sirhind Brigade, which had recently arrived from Egypt, forming the third brigade of the Lahore Division, was attacking north-east of Givenchy, on the left of the Ferozepore Brigade. In the fighting on the 16th the Ferozepore Brigade had suffered heavily, and the 59th Scinde Rifles from the Jullundur Brigade were lent to it temporarily. The 9th Bhopal Infantry rejoined on the 18th. The night of December 19th-20th passed without any marked incident, but at dawn the enemy opened a heavy fire with artillery and trench mortars along the whole of the Indian Corps' front. This was followed up by attacks against Givenchy.

At about 9 a.m. on the 20th a series of explosions took place along the trenches held by the Sirhind Brigade, where evidently the enemy had succeeded in mining under the parapet. Shortly after 1 p.m. the 129th Baluchis fell back and Givenchy was heavily attacked. The retention of this village was vital, as near this point the right of the Lahore Division connected with the left of the French. The enemy succeeded in driving the Sirhind Brigade from their trenches and occupied the whole of their front line ; the trenches on the left of the Ferozepore Brigade were also lost.

Operations of No. 1 Company.

It will now be necessary to turn to the 9th Bhopal Infantry and follow their fortunes in more detail. In this operation the Battalion was split up, as it was required to fill two gaps. One company, consisting of Sikhs and Rajputs under the command of Captains Cavendish and Dempster, with the machine guns under Lieutenant Balfour, was located in the support trenches on the left of the Ferozepore Brigade and next to the Sirhind Brigade. During the 18th and 19th this company supported the attack of the 59th Rifles against the enemy's sap heads. On December 20th, at about 11 a.m., Captain Cavendish heard that the enemy had succeeded in driving in the Sirhind Brigade on his left, and was ordered to move forward and protect the left flank. As the company was moving up, Captain Cavendish was wounded, later dying of his wounds. In him the Battalion lost an excellent officer; he was always cheery and knew how to command. Captain Dempster then took command and finding the front line trenches to his immediate front unoccupied manned them. The Germans at that moment delivered a strong attack. Captain Dempster was wounded and his company lost their way in the strange trenches. Lieutenant Balfour collected about thirty of the survivors and attached himself to the 129th Baluchis. Fighting went on all day; in the evening orders were given to withdraw, and Lieutenant Balfour accordingly retired with his handful of men to Le Quesnoy. Captain Dempster was taken prisoner and subsequently died of his wounds. He was a very gallant officer, full of initiative. The Battalion greatly deplored his loss

Operations of No. 2 Company.

Meanwhile, the second company, consisting of Muhammadans and Brahmins under Captain Jardine and Lieutenants Fasken and Taylor, were holding a portion of the line with the 57th Wilde's Rifles.

During the 18th and 19th this company had a comparatively peaceful time, but during the heavy attack on the 20th it was very much occupied. The 57th Rifles were holding the centre section of the Brigade line. The enemy succeeded in capturing the fire trench and in driving the defenders back to the supporting company furnished by the 9th Bhopal Infantry. Captain Jardine, correctly appreciating the situation, immediately threw up a barricade in the communication trench; this prevented the Germans from rushing into his trench, although they made repeated efforts to do so, every effort was frustrated. Captain Jardine was ably supported by Lieutenant Deedes, who was with the 57th Wilde's Rifles, and commanded their machine guns.

In the afternoon the Germans ceased to attempt to force this barricade, and the situation became quieter. Captain Jardine reconnoitred to his front and found that for at least 100 yards the enemy had withdrawn. Not having sufficient men to hold this line of trench permanently, he asked for more men to be sent up and in answer to his appeal some French infantry came up and occupied the vacant trench. The 57th Wilde's Rifles were removed elsewhere, but Captain Jardine held on to his piece of ground repelling all further attacks during December 21st and 22nd. During the night of the 22nd-23rd the South Staffords relieved him, and at 8.30 a.m. on the 23rd he returned with his company to billets at Béthune. This company, by holding on its ground, lost only one man killed and fourteen wounded. The company had put up a very fine show and was deservedly congratulated by the Brigade Commander.

Describing the fighting round Givenchy, Sir James Willcocks, in "The Indian Corps in France," says :—

"Very little has hitherto been said about the work of the 57th Rifles and one company of the 9th Bhopals beyond mentioning the fact that they held their portion of the line throughout. The share taken by them deserves more detailed mention, as it was owing to their determination and tenacious grip of their trenches that communication with the French on their right was maintained, and that our line was kept intact in this section of the defence."

Sir John French, in his despatch of December 2nd, 1915, sums up his opinion of the work of the Indian Corps :—

"The Indian troops have fought with the utmost steadfastness and gallantry whenever they have been called upon."

After two months of constant fighting the Battalion badly required rest. Only a handful of the original personnel remained ; the reinforcements sent haphazardly required time to settle down. Officers from many units had joined the Battalion, and they were strangers to the men. On December 24th there is an entry in the Battalion diary to the effect thus :—

"Forty-six men were unable to march from Béthune to Beaupiere owing to frost-bite or swollen feet."

This form of sickness was due to wet and cold feet ; it was found later to be preventable with proper discipline and care. This could be done by keeping the feet well greased, boots removed when possible, dry socks, and puttees loosened to allow of free circulation.

Christmas Day was spent in a state of constant readiness, and was not a very happy one; the Battalion was still clothed in its thin Indian khaki drill, and the day was bitterly cold. From now onwards the reinforcements joined the Battalion trained in the new conditions of warfare in France—digging of trenches, handling and throwing of bombs, firing of rifle grenades, constructing wire entanglements, etc. On the 27th Major Thomas from the 44th Infantry joined and was posted permanent Second-in-Command. He brought with him more reinforcements consisting of 35 men from the 21st Punjabis, 43 men from the 1st Brahmins and 10 men from the Advanced Base who belonged to the Battalion. On December 28th General Sir Edmund Barrow visited the Battalion. On January 1st, 1915, Captain Wilson and Lieutenant Neale, both of the 1st Brahmins, joined. The weather now turned very wet and cold; there are several entries in the diary to the effect that the day was too wet for any work. Home leave for officers was opened, but stopped again on January 12th. On January 17th Captain Brock (I.M.S.) went sick. He had done sterling work while in medical charge, and the Battalion was exceedingly sorry to lose him. He died later in India. On the 19th further drafts were received—1 Indian officer and 24 men from the 21st Punjabis, 1 Indian officer and 49 men from the 4th Rajputs, 1 Indian officer and 53 men from the 18th Infantry. Cases of mumps began to occur amongst the men; this sickness went on for months, the Regiment never getting rid of it till it had left France.

December, 1914, and January, 1915.

On January 31st the Ferozepore Brigade was reconstituted with the following units. The 129th Baluchis, 125th Napier's Rifles, 2/8th Gurkhas and the 9th Bhopal Infantry. On this day the Battalion moved to La Perriere, where training was resumed as soon as troops had settled themselves down in their new surroundings. From this place the Brigade almost daily furnished working parties for the Meerut Division, which was holding the front line. On February 5th the machine gun section was attached to the Meerut Division. On the 9th Captain Burdett, 11th Rajputs, joined the Battalion, bringing with him a complete company from that regiment (strength: 4 Indian officers and 155 other ranks). This was a very welcome reinforcement, and the men worked

La Perriere.

splendidly all the time that they were with the Battalion. On February 22nd the machine gun section rejoined.

Training in Reserve.

General Sir James Willcocks always took a great interest in his troops by paying them frequent visits and talking to the Indian officers with whom he was well acquainted. He paid the Battalion a visit on the 25th. These few weeks of training were of the utmost value, allowing the drafts to settle down and the officers and men to get to know one another. Nevertheless, Major Carleton's task in welding together the numerous reinforcements into a homogeneous unit was no light one, as the training was frequently interrupted by calls for other duties. At the beginning of March the following British officers were present :—

Major Carleton (Commanding), Major Thomas (Second-in-Command), Captains Jardine, Burdett, Wilson, Kirkwood, 97th Infantry, who joined on March 6th, Martin (Adjutant), Lieutenants Balfour, Taylor, Fasken, Neale and Banks. In the place of Captain Brock (I.M.S.), the Medical Officer, Captain C. H. Wright (I.M.S.) was appointed.

On March 7th the Battalion was moved to a new area at Calonne and was held in a state of readiness. It soon became evident from the preparations already in training in this area that large scale operations were about to begin.

The period of training was drawing to a close, and the second and more successful battle for Neuve Chapelle was about to take place. The Battalion was reinforced on the 7th with a new draft of 1 Indian officer and 25 men from the 21st Punjabis, 1 Indian officer and 36 men from the 18th Infantry, and 7 men of the 11th Rajputs rejoined from the base.

The Second Battle of Neuve Chapelle.

Since October, 1914, the village of Neuve Chapelle had been in German hands, and formed a salient which it was very desirable to straighten out. These operations were entrusted to the Indian Corps. Prior to the beginning of the battle the 9th Bhopal Infantry was withdrawn from the Ferozepore Brigade and placed directly under the command of Corps Headquarters, by whom it was employed on a variety of duties. On March 8th Major Thomas took two companies to Fosse, and worked independently of the Battalion for the next three days. On the 10th two platoons were used as escort for prisoners at Robecque. Battalion

Headquarters moved to Les Lobes and another two platoons were required at Lacon for loading ammunition. On the 12th the Battalion reassembled at La Couture. On the 13th it moved to the Chateau de Fosse, from here the machine gun section was sent to the Sirhind Brigade and was away till March 25th. Companies were now employed on duties such as road-repairing, clearing the battlefield, entrenching, etc. On the 18th the reserve machine gun section was sent to the Jullundur Brigade. On the 27th General Sir James Willcocks paid one of his periodic visits while the Battalion was at Pacut, and expressed himself very pleased with everything he saw

On the 28th the Battalion rejoined the Ferozepore Brigade. For three weeks the Battalion had been engaged on a number of tasks and, although it did not take part in any of the actual fighting for Neuve Chapelle, it was actively and usefully employed. On the 30th Major O'Reilly, 63rd Infantry, joined, but was only with the Battalion for a few days before he was transferred. On the 31st the Battalion took over a portion of the line north of Neuve Chapelle, with two companies up and two companies at Croix Barbee. During the next few days everything was very quiet on this front; the two companies in the trenches were relieved on April 2nd, and the Battalion moved to Paradis. Whilst in these billets occasional heavy shelling took place which caused a certain number of casualties daily. Swollen feet still gave trouble amongst the men, but with proper care and attention, this was gradually being overcome. There was now more time for training, and both the Brigade and the Battalion were able to carry out practice attacks. On April 19th a draft of 1 Indian officer and 45 men arrived from the 5th Light Infantry. This was a very poor draft, the men had not attained the same standard of training reached by previous reinforcements, nor were the men of the same quality.

It was understood that the Lahore Division was to take over the front from the Meerut Division, but, very suddenly on April 24th, just as orders for the relief of the Meerut Division had been issued, the Lahore Division, with utmost dispatch, was sent to Ypres, where a very serious situation had arisen.

CHAPTER XI.

SECOND BATTLE OF YPRES.

In order to make clear the general situation, it will be necessary to give a very brief account of what was happening north of Ypres, and why the Lahore Division had to move so suddenly to the assistance of General Smith-Dorrien's Second Army.

General Situation.

On April 22nd, General Sir H. Plumer, commanding the V Corps, was holding two-thirds of the southern portion of the front of the salient, covering Ypres with the 27th, 28th and Canadian Divisions. The third portion was being occupied by the French. These allied forces were practically on the line where the fighting had come to an end on November 11th, 1914. The Canadian Division held that portion of the line next to the French, the Poelcappelle road dividing them. The 45th Algerian Division, consisting of coloured troops, held the right portion of the French line.

Gas Attacks by the Germans.

April 22nd was a glorious spring day. In the forenoon there was considerable shelling of Ypres by 17-inch, 11-inch and 8-inch howitzers, but this gradually ceased. At 5 p.m. a new and furious bombardment of the whole line by heavy and light howitzers recommenced. Suddenly some officers observed two curious greenish yellow clouds on the ground on either side of Langemarck. Behind these clouds the enemy was advancing. Soon a peculiar smell, accompanied by smarting of the eyes and tingling of the nose and throat was noticed. It was some little time before it was realized that the yellow clouds were due to poison gas, and almost simultaneously French coloured troops without officers began drifting down the roads, through the back areas of the V Corps. It was impossible to understand what these Africans said, but from the way they coughed and pointed to their throats, it was evident that, if not actually suffering from the effects of gas, they were thoroughly scared. Teams and wagons of French artillery next retired, and the stream of fugitives rapidly increased. The French seventy-fives were firing away until 7 p.m., when they suddenly ceased. Immediately the attack took place the Canadians moved up their reserves as their left flank was in grave danger of envelopment. The French left a gap of four miles which was held only at three points. The V Corps then organized a series of counter-attacks, followed later by further counter-attacks under the Second Army. These reserves were used up in trying to fill the gap caused by the withdrawal of the French.

Demand for the Lahore Division.

On the morning of the 24th fresh gas operations were opened against the Canadians. Wave after wave of the enemy came up against them, the gas-cloud having risen to fifteen feet high, and the Canadians had no protection whatsoever, except a wet handkerchief or a towel. Many were overcome and collapsed, but the majority succeeded in manning the parapet and beating off the enemy. Eventually with all their reserves used up in the filling of the French gap, these plucky Canadians had to withdraw to avoid being surrounded. There were no further reserves to help them, and they fell back fighting every yard of the ground. This was the situation which caused the urgent demand for the Lahore Division, and it was into this battle that the Indian troops, unprotected against gas, were to be hurled.

Attack by the Lahore Division.

The Lahore Division had reached Ouderdom on April 25th, after heavy marching. At 5.30 a.m. on the 26th the Division left its billets; its three infantry brigades were under strength owing to sickness and lack of reinforcements. The Jullundur and Ferozepore Brigades, passing close by Ypres, reached their places of assembly near St. Jean at 11 a.m., though not without suffering some loss from artillery fire on the way. At 12.30 p.m. the brigades moved up to the place of deployment and formed up, the Jullundur Brigade on the right and the Ferozepore on the left, just north of La Brique. Their orders were to attack northwards. The 129th Baluchis were on the right of the Ferozepore Brigade, the 57th Rifles in the centre and the Connaught Rangers on the left. The 4th Londons and the 9th Bhopal Infantry were in support. The French were to co-operate on the left of the Connaughts. At the critical moment, 2.20 p.m., just as the leading British attackers had actually reached the wire, the Germans released gas opposite the right French battalion. Drifting across the front of the Ferozepore Brigade, the cloud checked the advance everywhere, whilst the enemy redoubled his fire. The Indian troops, who were without any means of protection, suffered very heavily and fell back in confusion. At night the Jullundur and Ferozepore Brigades were relieved by the Sirhind Brigade, which immediately consolidated the line.

Attack on April 27th.

On the 27th arrangements had been made to attack with the French, the Lahore Division co-operating. The Ypres—Langemarck road remained, as before, the boundary between the two. Orders were therefore issued that the Ferozepore Brigade from between St. Jean and La Brique should advance at 12.30 p.m. and come up on the right of the Sirhind Brigade. The two brigades would then move forward simultaneously with the French. The Sirhind Brigade did not wait, but, taking advantage of the bombardment, moved forward as soon as it commenced. The Ferozepore Brigade, reduced to 38 British officers and 1,648 rifles, of which the three Indian battalions furnished only 688, also moved off at 12.30 p.m. from St. Jean. It met with a heavy fire as soon as it came over the ridge, but pressed on until abreast of the Sirhind Brigade, when it was held up.

In this attack the 9th Bhopal Infantry were on the right and the 4th Londons on the left ; in support were the Connaughts, 57th Rifles and 129th Baluchis. In the advance Major Jamieson was wounded and Captain Etlenger (acting Adjutant for the day) fell mortally wounded.

All the morning Second Army Headquarters had been endeavouring to find a brigade to support the Lahore Division. This proved impossible, as every formation was reduced in numbers, and eventually a composite brigade was collected, but no stronger than one battalion. Another attack was planned for 5.30 p.m., but before the British were ready, the French on the left advanced ; this attack withered away before it had gone very far. At 6.30 p.m. another attack was made by the two Indian brigades, which the Germans met with a terrific burst of fire of all kinds. There was hope that the leading lines would get to their objective, when suddenly word was passed that gas had been turned on the Turcos and that they were fleeing in panic. The Africans were seen crowding back and were only stopped by some French troops in the rear. In consequence of this orders were issued by the Second Army to consolidate the ground ; the survivors of the attack were brought back to the line held in the morning. The Germans did not pursue, but left their opponents in peace to organize and clear up the battlefield. During the operations the 9th Bhopal Infantry lost three British officers, Captain Etlenger, mortally wounded, Major Jamieson and Captain Kirkwood, wounded, and 2 Indian officers and 117 men. The loss of Captain Etlenger was a very serious one. He was a very popular officer with everyone, a fine commander of men, never pessimistic even on the worst occasions, always a cheery companion, and in fact a first-rate soldier. In addition to this, he was a thorough sportsman, a good cricketer and excelled at all games.

On April 28th the enemy made no attacks. The Lahore Division had been ordered to consolidate its line, and reconnaissances to the front showed that a more forward line could be taken up; eventually this line was dug and wired. Although it was bright moonlight, the Germans were so occupied with their own wiring that they did not hinder the British wiring parties. On completion of the work the Lahore Division handed over to the 13th Brigade.

It will be of interest here to mention that at one time on the 28th Sir John French seriously thought of giving up the Ypres salient, and ordered General Sir H. Plumer to take preliminary measures for commencing the retirement, should this prove necessary. General Foch protested vehemently against any thought of withdrawal; in the words of the official account, General Foch stated, "That the lost ground could be retaken with the troops already available; that to withdraw was to invite the enemy to come on and repeat his attack, and that to win a second battle it was not necessary to lose a first." He begged Sir John French before giving orders for retirement to wait until he had seen the results of the French attacks to be made next day. To this the British Field-Marshal agreed. It will be seen therefore, that a very serious situation had arisen and disaster was only averted by the gallantry of the troops who defended the salient during those critical days.

During the night April 29th-30th the Ferozepore and Sirhind Brigades withdrew to Ouderdom. The Divisional Commander, in his report on the operations, states:—

"I consider the troops did all that it was humanly possible to do under most trying circumstances. They had to pass under a hail of shell fire, advance to a position of assembly over open ground, and from thence to a position of deployment under the same conditions."

The Battalion moves Southward.

On the 30th, at 9.30 a.m., the Battalion started its march southwards, and after having gone a couple of miles was ordered to halt. It spent the rest of the day in a field hiding from the enemy's aeroplanes, which were very active. In the evening it returned to Ouderdom. On May 1st at 6.30 p.m. orders were received to move south, and on the 2nd the Battalion reached Doulieu. At this place Captain Ralston joined the Battalion and took over the duties of Adjutant from Captain Martin, who took over No. 1 Company. The Battalion then moved to Paradis, where it went into billets only to prepare for another big attack near Neuve Chapelle. This time the attack was to be carried out by the Meerut Division with the Lahore Division in close support.

General Sir H. Plumer sent the following message to the troops of the Lahore Division :—

" Will you please convey to the brigadiers, commanding officers and all officers, non-commissioned officers and men of your Division my thanks for the assistance they have rendered in the recent severe fighting, and my appreciation of the way in which they have carried out the very arduous duties entrusted to them while under my command. I deeply regret the very heavy casualties they have suffered."

Organization of the Battalion.

On May 4th the Battalion was organized into Headquarters and three companies. No. 1 Company, consisting of Sikhs of the 9th Bhopals and 21st Punjabis, Rajputs of the 4th Rajputs and 16th Rajputs ; No. 2 Company, Muhammadans of the 9th, 17th, 18th Infantry and 19th Punjabis ; No. 3 Company, 11th Rajputs and men of the 8th Infantry, 89th Punjabis, 96th Berar Infantry and Brahmins of the 89th Punjabis and 1st Brahmins. This gives some idea of the difficulties with which the Battalion had to contend in absorbing the reinforcements sent them. While fighting was in progress, it was a very difficult problem to mould these drafts into a fighting machine and to get officers, Indian officers, non-commissioned officers and men acquainted with each other.

On May 6th the Battalion was issued with gas masks for the first time. This consisted of a flannel head-cover with eye-holes, the flannel being saturated with an anti-gas mixture.

CHAPTER XII

OPERATIONS DURING MAY, 1915.

THE British and French Higher Commands had planned offensives which were to take place simultaneously early in May—the French attack being in the direction of Lens, and the British north of the La Bassée Canal, with the object of gaining the Aubers Ridge. The Indian Corps was to cover the left of the I Corps and capture Ferme du Biez. This offensive should have taken place soon after the middle of April, and secret instructions had been issued to this effect, but these operations had to be held in abeyance until the situation at Ypres had become more secure. The enemy may have had some indication that offensive operations were in progress, as on May 1st, the whole of the rearward portion of the Indian Corps area was subjected to a heavy bombardment.

General Situation.

On May 6th the Lahore Division took over the front held by the Meerut Division. The original attack was planned for May 8th, but this was postponed for twenty-four hours. On May 9th, therefore, at 5 a.m., the enemy's front line was bombarded for forty minutes, at the end of which the troops detailed by the Meerut Division attacked. It was at once discovered that the forty minutes' bombardment had not had the slightest effect on the enemy, who manned their parapet ready to receive the attack. A deadly machine-gun fire opened all along the line, and it was not many minutes before the survivors of the attacking troops of the Meerut Division were back in their trenches again. It was quite evident that our attack had been a complete failure. The German guns now opened a heavy bombardment on the whole front line, and communication trenches. The attack of the 1st Division on the right of the Indian Corps was similarly held up. On the left the 8th British Division met with some success. Later in the morning it was observed that the enemy were massing and a counter-attack appeared imminent. Reinforcements were immediately sent forward, but with wounded men returning and reinforcements moving up, the communication trenches became so congested that

Attack by the Meerut Division.

it was almost impossible to move in them. In "The Indian Corps in France," Sir James Willcocks thus describes the scene :—

"These trenches, difficult to pass through, even when occupied only by the ordinary traffic, were now in a state which beggars description. The German guns had been pounding high explosive and shrapnel into them all the morning. In many places the parapet had been blown in, blocking the way, while numbers of dead and wounded were lying at the bottom of the trenches. The direction boards had in many cases been destroyed, and men were wandering about, vainly attempting to find the nearest way to their units, or to the aid posts. The nearer one got to the front, the more of a shambles the trenches became—wounded men were creeping and crawling along amidst the mud and debris of the parapet, many of them unable to extricate themselves, dying alone and unattended, whilst amidst this infernal scene the German shells were continually bursting."

The first assault having completely failed, two more were planned during the day, but had to be abandoned owing to the confusion in the trenches.

Meanwhile, the 9th Bhopal Infantry was taking its part—a quiet one this time—in this unsuccessful fight. On May 8th the Battalion had been moved to the orchard close to Neuve Chapelle — the scene of the fighting in October, 1914, arriving there at midnight.

Activities of the Battalion.

The Battalion then moved forward and occupied some fire trenches adjoining a spot known as Port Arthur, close to the La Bassée road. The night was a quiet one, and the Battalion occupied its position without any casualties. As soon as the Meerut Division assault had failed, the German guns commenced to pound our front line, now somewhat crowded. Casualties soon became numerous. One shell buried four British officers, Major Carleton, Major Thomas, Captain Ralston and Captain Martin ; the latter was only slightly bruised and able to carry on, but the three former were completely knocked out and had to be carried away. Major Carleton's command thus came to an end. He had been with the Battalion through some of its hardest fighting and had an uphill task in pulling the Battalion together after its trying ordeal. It was therefore with great regret that his services were now lost. He did not recover for months, and was then later severely wounded again whilst commanding his own battalion in Mesopotamia. Major Thomas was completely incapacitated and was unable to rejoin for over six months, when he took over command of the Battalion in Mesopotamia at one of the worst periods. Unfortunately he did not long survive, dying of wounds sustained while gallantly leading his men in the charge.

Lance-Naik Angad Pande.

A number of gallant acts were performed on this day (May 9th). Amongst them was the plucky work of No. 2,869 Lance-Naik Angad Pande. His duty was at Ferozepore Brigade Headquarters. The Brigade was anxious to know the situation on our front as, owing to the enemy's bombardment, communication between us and them had been severed. The communication trenches were blocked. Lance-Naik Angad Pande volunteered to find the headquarters of the Battalion and deliver the message. He ran several hundred yards across the open under shell, rifle and machine-gun fire, found Battalion Headquarters in the front line trench and delivered his message. How he escaped is a miracle, and he fully deserved the Indian Distinguished Service Medal which he was immediately awarded.

On this day, besides the three British officers wounded, 1 Indian officer and 39 other ranks became casualties. During May 10th no further attacks took place. That evening the Battalion was withdrawn into billets at Riez Bailleil. 2nd-Lieutenant B. Hayfield, I.A.R.O., joined the Battalion, the first Indian Army Reserve Officer to join the 9th Bhopal Infantry. From the 11th to the 14th the Battalion remained in these billets. 2nd-Lieutenant E. Cameron Ker, I.A.R.O., joined on the 12th.

On the 15th the Battalion took over some trenches close to Neuve Chapelle and occupied them until May 22nd, when it received orders to proceed to Egypt. It was a remarkable coincidence that the Battalion concluded its fighting in France on the identical spot where it had fought its first battle on October 27th and 28th, 1914. Of the original Battalion, the only fit survivors were Captain Martin and a handful of men.

On May 19th Major Samborne-Palmer, 8th Rajputs, had joined and assumed command, *vice* Captain Jardine, who had taken over command as soon as Major Carleton was wounded.

On the 24th the Battalion entrained at Lestrem, together with the 125th Napier's Rifles. Before entraining, General Sir J. Willcocks and Major-General D'U. Keary, commanding the Lahore Division, came to wish the Battalion "good-bye," and to thank the men for all the work that they had done.

FAREWELL ORDER BY MAJOR-GENERAL D'U. KEARY, COMMANDING THE LAHORE DIVISION.

"In view of the departure of the 9th Bhopal Infantry from his command, the General Officer Commanding the Division wishes to acknowledge the excellent work done by the Battalion which has taken its part in several great battles in a war that has produced the greatest battles the world has ever seen. It has borne itself with gallantry and devotion to duty.

"Its losses have been severe, but its morale has been maintained through all vicissitudes, while its discipline and good conduct have at all times been of the best.

"The G.O.C. wishes to thank Major Carleton and the officers who have been under his command for such a record and to assure all ranks of his appreciation of their services.

"He wishes them farewell with a hope that all good fortune may attend the Battalion in such further part as they may take in the World-wide War."

Departure from France.

The 9th Bhopal Infantry arrived at Marseilles on the 26th and camped on the Race Course in the same spot where it had pitched its camp at the end of September, 1914. The Regiment was relieved by the 89th Punjabis. On June 5th the Battalion embarked on the ss. *Elephanta* for Port Said. Strength: 9 British officers, 9 Indian officers, 752 other ranks.

Just before embarking, Captain Burdett was ordered to join the 89th Punjabis. He had originally come with his own company from the 11th Rajputs and had joined the Battalion in January. His own men deeply felt parting with him; they volunteered to return to the trenches in France and continue to serve under him. This incident is small in itself, but there is a great principle underlying it, for it shows the true spirit of relationship between the British officer and his men—a close comradeship which hardships and war merely strengthen. It was not possible to grant their request and the men were broken-hearted at parting with him. A few weeks later he was killed with the 89th Punjabis. Captain Burdett was a splendid type of regimental officer, always cheery and blest with a sense of humour ; keen on his men, looking always to their comfort, a strict disciplinarian and a first-class soldier.

This, then, ends the story of the Battalion in France. The 9th Bhopal Infantry had landed in September, 1914, as one unit, by June, 1915, it consisted of many units. To make these drafts into one unit again and into an efficient fighting machine, training and reorganization was required. Time was to be given it in Egypt to carry this out, and after a few months it was ready to take the field again, this time in Mesopotamia.

It will not be out of place here to mention a few of the lessons that were learnt in France.

Lessons learnt in France.

The outstanding question was one of efficient reinforcements. Before the war it had not been foreseen that these would be required in such large numbers. The reservists were of little use, and the Depot was unable to meet requirements. Steps have since been taken to remedy this, and the new system is an immense improvement on the old—but it has yet to stand the test of war. The second lesson learned is the principle of keeping a proportion of experienced officers, non-commissioned officers and specialists out of the fight to serve as a nucleus for the future. In the early days of the war this would have been difficult to any appreciable extent, but at the same time the principle should have been observed.

The third lesson which was proved as the war went on was, that none but the very best class of Indian troops is fit for European war, and then only when led by a sufficient number of experienced British officers.

This leads to the last lesson—the British officer. In fighting against European armies organized on similar lines, his presence is of paramount importance, and has a direct bearing on the fighting efficiency of the Indian soldier. But he must be of the right type. When battalions were depleted of their British officers efficiency declined immediately. In his book, "The Indian Corps in France," from which previous quotations have been made, Sir James Willcocks has much to say on this subject, of which the following is quoted :—

"It soon happened that many battalions lost every officer who, in far away India, had instructed them in the military art, and who, in the eyes of the Indian troops, were all that remained to remind them, with familiar authority, of their homes and their duty. They felt their bereavement as orphans, old enough to realize their sorrow, and to feel it. Every ingenuity and every conceivable resource was exhausted by the authorities in the attempt to supply new officers to take the place of the fallen. A constant succession of gallant young gentlemen was drafted from India and from home to fill the gaps in the ranks. But it was not possible to keep pace completely with the losses. And even when the numbers were forthcoming, there was hardly leisure to establish in the necessary degree acquaintance and confidence. This could have mattered little in a British regiment. Provided his officer is competent, considerate and brave, the British soldier can support many changes and institutions in his commands. No such adaptability can be expected, and little is in fact found, among the Indian battalions. Foremost, therefore, among the trials and the difficulties which the Indian troops had to bear, and to which in the main they proved stoically equal, were the cruel losses of officers to whom they had become devoted, and whom they had been in the habit of following through any dangers to any objective."

The following figures relating to the 9th Bhopal Infantry are of interest :—

(*a*) The field service scale of the Battalion when it landed in France was :—13 British officers, 18 Indian officers, 807 Indian other ranks. Of these 1 Indian officer and 72 other ranks were "first reinforcements."

(*b*) Battle casualties amounted to 708.

(*c*) Sick numbered 569, of whom 430 included lightly wounded returned to the field.

(*d*) Deaths from other causes, 6, mostly pneumonia.

(*e*) Medical unfits, 27. These were men who joined in the field but were not up to standard.

(*f*) Reinforcements were received as follows :—

GENERAL MAP OF NORTHERN FRANCE

MAP No. 3

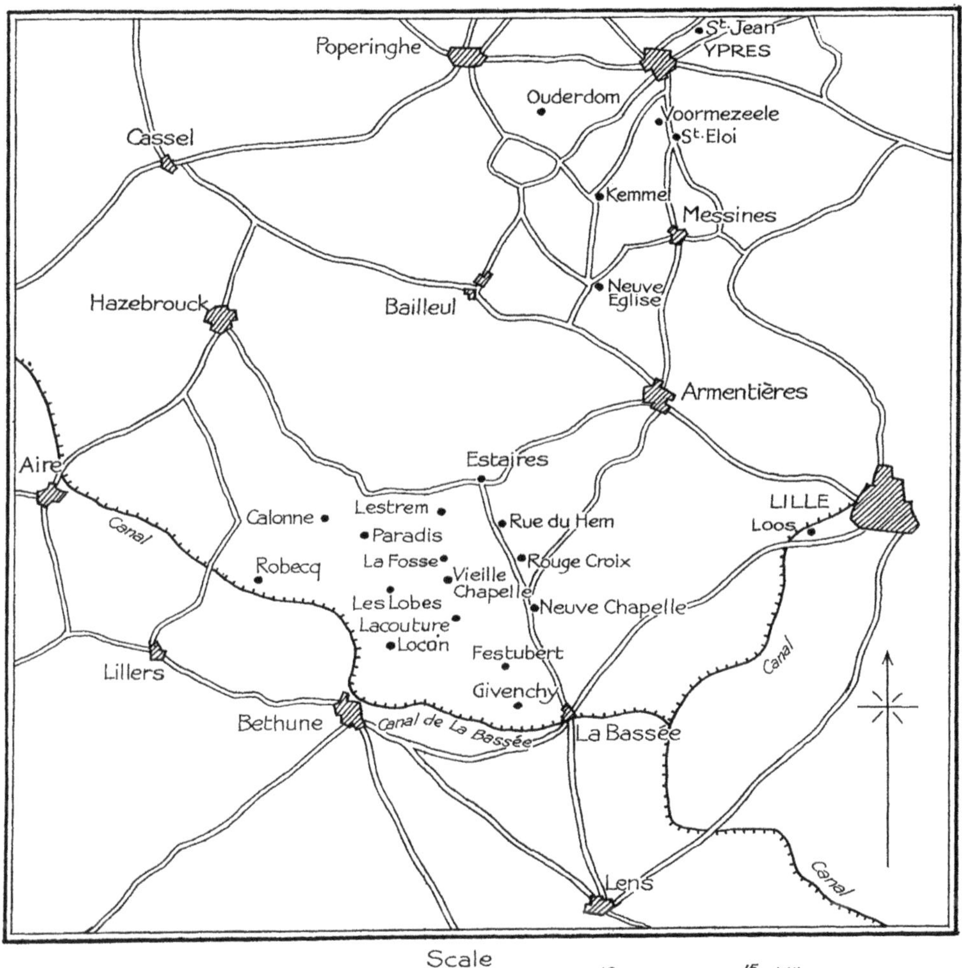

	Indian Officers.	*Indian Other Ranks.*
9th Infantry Depot	1	153
96th Infantry	1	69
21st Punjabis	2	105
1st Brahmins	—	60
4th Rajputs	1	49
18th Infantry	2	97
11th Rajputs	4	173
17th Infantry	1	56
5th Light Infantry	—	42
16th Rajputs	—	42
89th Punjabis	1	64
Total	13	910

Part III.
SERVICE IN EGYPT.

CHAPTER XIII

SERVICE IN EGYPT

THE Battalion, together with 300 men of the 125th Napier's Rifles, embarked on the s.s. *Elephanta* by noon on June 5th.

Voyage to Port Said.

The following officers were present:—Major F. C. Samborne-Palmer, Commanding; Captains C. H. Jardine and G. D. Martin; Lieutenants G. Balfour, Neale, B. W. Browning, Cameron Ker, Hayfield, with Lieutenant M. Das, I.M.S., in medical charge. The Battalion embarked with 9 British officers, 9 Indian officers and 752 other ranks. At 4 p.m. the ship put in at Toulon, and stayed the night there, sailing at 9 a.m. next day.

Hostile submarines had already appeared in the Mediterranean, necessitating precautions to be taken to meet an emergency. The ship carried no guns, so reliance had to be placed on rifle and machine-gun fire. The men were practised daily at their alarm stations; no lights were permitted, and an inlying picquet of 100 rifles had always to be ready to engage any submarine which might come within range. The voyage was uneventful, and on June 12th Port Said was reached. At this place the Battalion heard that its destination was Suez. Troops were ordered to disembark and proceed by rail. Leaving Port Said at 3.30 p.m., the Battalion reached its camp at Suez at 9.30 p.m. The Battalion now formed part of the 28th F.F. Brigade, commanded by Major-General Sir G. Younghusband.

At this time of the year it is warm under canvas at Suez, but the nights are cool. After the strenuous life they had led in France, the men enjoyed the comparative freedom and relaxation. The Battalion required to be reorganized, as many drafts had joined at Marseilles. A number of the men were unfit for further active service and required weeding out There was plenty of time in Suez for these details; Major Samborne-Palmer devoted himself to refitting the Battalion and making it once more a fighting unit. No. 1 Company was composed of Sikhs and Rajputs, No. 2 Company Muhammadans, No. 3 Company Rajputs, and No. 4 Company Muhammadans and Brahmins. Over one hundred men were found unfit

Reorganization.

and transferred to India or convalescent depots in Egypt. Towards the end of the month the Battalion received orders to take over a sector of the Canal Defences, in relief of the 56th Rifles Frontier Force. This was carried out on June 30th and July 1st.

The Situation on the Suez Canal.

It will not be out of place here to give a very short account of the military situation just prior to the arrival of the Battalion on the Canal Defences. The situation in Egypt was always a cause of anxiety, and the Suez Canal especially so as its security was vital to our Empire. The authorities had good reason for anxiety, as the following instances will show. On February 3rd, 1915, the Turks, led by German officers, made a very determined effort to reach Egypt with a force estimated at 25,000. Parts of this force reached the Canal, and some portion of it actually crossed to the west bank. The attack was easily repelled with heavy loss to the Turks, but it showed that large forces could be moved across the desert.

On March 22nd a patrol of the 56th Rifles near the port of El Kubri was fired on, losing a few men. On April 8th a hostile patrol appeared before Kantara, and later a mine was found in the Canal. On April 28th more Turkish detachments approached the Canal; these were discovered by patrols of the Bikanir Camel Corps, and the "movable column" marched out and engaged them. On May 3rd a party of about twenty Turks appeared opposite Ballah and Ferdain, and subsequently a mine was discovered buried in the sand. On the night of June 2nd-3rd the outposts near Kantara were shelled. On June 30th a Holt liner struck a mine in the Little Bitter Lake, despite the fact that the lake had been regularly patrolled by armed launches. This blocked the passage of the Canal for several hours.

These instances show that a continual watch was necessary to prevent the Turks attaining their object—namely, to block the Canal. This required, from the troops employed on the Canal Defences, constant patrolling and vigilance. The whole length of the Canal was divided into three sections, one from Suez to the Bitter Lakes, the centre section from the Great Bitter Lake to Ferdain, the northern section from Ferdain to Port Said. Force Headquarters and a reserve were at Ismailia. The defensive works on the Canal consisted of a series of posts protected by barbed wire on the east bank. All day long sentries watched the country to the east, and all night patrols moved between the posts. Before dawn the Bikanir Camel Corps, which had detachments in most of the posts, sent out patrols several miles to scour the country.

Defensive Precautions.

The Battalion, on taking over its section, adopted still further precautions. Before dark a large bush several feet wide was dragged by a mule from one post to the next, thus making a clear road on which any footprint could be at once seen. In the morning a mounted British officer rode along this road and examined it carefully for footprints. The relief of the southern section of the Canal Defences was completed by July 1st. The men's time was now employed in carrying out improvements in the posts and in various forms of training. The Battalion's section contained three posts, two of which were manned by 120 rifles and the third by 319 rifles. No sooner had the 56th Rifles been relieved than the 28th Brigade was on July 13th ordered to proceed to Aden. The 9th Bhopal Infantry was now transferred to the Imperial Service Brigade, commanded by Major-General Watson ; this brigade took over the Canal defences, held by the 28th F.F Brigade. The following officers joined the Battalion on July 27th :—Lieutenants Morrison and Roberts (both I.A.R.O.) ; and on the 28th Captain H. H. Smith and Second-Lieutenant F. L. Woledge, I.A.R.O.

The Battalion still had the remnants of the drafts received from various units whilst in France. Of these all men of the 16th Rajputs, 17th Infantry and 26th Punjabis were now returned to their own units, the only ones remaining being those from the 5th Infantry, 11th Rajputs, 21st Punjabis and the Burma Military Police.

Reconnoitring Parties.

The usual routine in the section was alternatively a month in posts and a month in the support area in New Camp, Suez. While in the posts there were frequent opportunities for swimming, and aquatic sports were occasionally organized. Beyond this there was little to relieve the monotony of leisure hours. On two occasions comparatively large reconnoitring parties were sent out. The first consisted of one troop Patiala Lancers, 10 Camel sowars and 100 rifles, and its object was to reconnoitre the ground in the vicinity of Bir Mabeuik and report on the well there. On arrival in the afternoon of November 17th, the Lancers made an extended reconnaissance while the infantry prepared a defensive position near the well for the night. A few shots were fired about midnight by wandering Arabs, but no damage was done and no trace of the firers could be found. The return march was begun shortly after daylight, and the party was back on the canal by noon. On December 1st a second and larger reconnoitring party visited the same place. This time there were rumours of the well being occupied, or at least visited by the enemy. The Column, which consisted of 400 rifles from the Battalion, left No. 3 Post (Kabrit) at 8.30 p.m. and returned by 6.30 p.m. on the 2nd. Nothing was seen of the enemy, and no trace was found of anyone having visited Bir Mabeuik since the previous reconnaissance.

This ended our period of service in Egypt. The six months spent in this country was devoted almost entirely to re-organization and training. This period was the most peaceful one the Battalion was destined to experience throughout the whole of the war.

Part IV.

SERVICE IN MESOPOTAMIA.

CHAPTER XIV

DURING 1915 the progress of the campaign in Mesopotamia had been so favourable that the leaders on the spot were very sanguine of capturing Baghdad if given two more Divisions. These the Indian Government were unwilling to spare from India, but agreed to send the two Divisions recently withdrawn from the French front. Meanwhile the 6th Indian Division had been sent to effect the capture of Baghdad single-handed. At first all went well, but at Ctesiphon its advance was checked and it was forced to retire on Kut-al-Amara, where eventually it was besieged. In view of this reverse, the early dispatch of two extra Divisions became urgently necessary.

Departure from Egypt.

The 9th Bhopal Infantry, as part of the 7th Division, embarked at Suez on December 5th on the H.T. *Nizam* for Basra. The Battalion's strength was 12 British officers, 16 Indian officers and 881 rank and file.

The British officers were Lieutenant-Colonel Samborne-Palmer; Major G. A. Jamieson; Captain H. H. Smith; Brevet-Major C. H. Jardine; Captain G. D. Martin, M.C.; Lieutenants R. S. Banks, A. Cameron Ker, F. L. Woledge, P. M. McSwiney, W. H. Morrison, F. C. Roberts; and Lieutenant M. Das, I.M.S. A halt of a few hours was made at Aden to take on supplies for the further voyage to Basra. There news was received of the Battle of Ctesiphon and of the death in action of Lieutenant-Colonel C. C. Jackson, Commanding the 103rd Maharattas. This officer had done nearly all his service with the 9th Bhopal Infantry and had only left in 1912 to take up the appointment of Second-in-Command of the 101st Grenadiers. He was a favourite with all ranks, and his death was very deeply regretted by all who knew him.

Arrival at Basra.

The Battalion reached Basra about 1.30 p.m., December 21st, and commenced disembarkation at about 4 p.m. Owing to lack of facilities only personnel were disembarked that day, and the last of the men were not ashore until 9 p.m. That night was spent in a rest camp and the ship was unloaded by 10 a.m. on the 22nd. Kits were found to be heavier than the regulations allowed on account of the liberal gifts received by the men both in France and Egypt; but now, owing to lack of transport, kits had of necessity to be cut down to below Field Service scale, and the balance dumped at an improvised depot. In addition to this, all unfits and insufficiently trained men had to be weeded out and left behind.

After much bustle, matters were satisfactorily settled, and the Battalion, less those detailed for the depot, embarked on the paddle steamer "P.S.4" at about 1 p.m. on the 22nd. The "P.S.4" moved up-stream to Nahr Umr, where the Battalion disembarked and bivouacked for the night. Here the Battalion joined the remainder of a force designated "B" Echelon, consisting of the 6th Jats, a composite Battalion of Maharattas, and about one company of British reinforcements, the two latter intended for the 6th Division.

The March up the Tigris.

At 11 a.m. on December 23rd. "B" Echelon marched off for Safi, arriving there at 3.30 p.m. As, however, maps were not issued, and place names existed in the minds of the imaginative and of non-resident Arabs, a considerable amount of ingenuity had to be exercised to discover where Safi actually was. On resuming the march next day it was discovered that the previous day's march had been underestimated by about an hour. At the real Safi the bridge was found to be broken, and Echelon "B" had to wait until it had been repaired, bivouacking that night near the bridge. The bridge was ready on Christmas Day, and "B" Echelon then crossed and went into bivouac about a mile further on, near the right bank of the Tigris, just beyond the outskirts of Qurna. Here it was joined by the 41st Dogras and a portion of the animals and wagons of the 7th Divisional Ammunition Column.

Little of interest occurred during the next four marches. Ezra's tomb and Qala Salih, however, whose buildings and trees made landmarks on an otherwise featureless horizon, aroused some little interest. From Ezra's Tomb the track led along a narrow strip between the river and the Shammar lake. The latter was the resting-place of countless flocks of waterfowl, and looked as perfect a spot for a Christmas camp as a party of sportsmen could wish. In Mesopotamia at this time of year sand grouse collect in flights, which must occasionally run into hundreds of thousands of birds. Many were the expressions of regret that Field Service scale did not admit of the carriage of suitable armament. On December 30th the Battalion arrived at Amara, where it lost the services of Lieutenant-Colonel Samborne-Palmer, ordered to rejoin his own battalion in the Persian Gulf, and Lieutenant Woledge, who accidentally wounded himself with his revolver and consequently was out of action for a short spell.

On January 4th the Echelon arrived at Ali-al-Garbi, where the force intended for the relief of Kut was concentrating. Here the Battalion was joined by Lieutenant-Colonel F. W. Thomas, who assumed command.

Situation on the Tigris Front.

At this time the situation was as follows :—The 6th Division, after its withdrawal from Ctesiphon, had retired as far as Kut, where General Townshend decided to stand in order to prevent the enemy advancing further down stream in any considerable force. Meanwhile the Turks had been reinforced, and later information indicated that further reinforcements were on their way from Gallipoli, where they were no longer required. By the middle of December the 6th Division was hemmed in the Kut peninsula, where, at that time, General Townshend reported that he had one month's provisions for British and two months for Indian troops. In these circumstances it was considered imperative that the relief force should advance on Kut at the earliest possible moment ; already rations in Kut must be running short.

On January 5th another echelon arrived at Ali-al-Gharbi, and the relief force comprised four Infantry Brigades, one Cavalry Brigade and one Brigade of Royal Field Artillery. The Battalion was now posted to the 21st Brigade, under Brigadier-General Norie, V.C., the other units being the Black Watch, the 9th Gurkhas, and the 41st Dogras.

The 3rd Division was on its way, and another Division, the 13th, was under orders to move to Mesopotamia. The situation of the 6th Division in Kut was such, however, that it was considered inadvisable to await the arrival of these two divisions before advancing to the relief of Kut.

On the morning of January 6th the relief force advanced, "B" Company, 9th Bhopal Infantry, acting as rearguard to the Brigade, which that day marched about twenty miles. That night rain fell in torrents, accompanied by bitterly cold winds. Except for a patch of ground here and there, the ground was soon under water. Under such circumstances sleep, or even rest, were impossible. Early next morning gun-fire could be heard, and the flashes of bursting shell were seen. From Basra to near Baghdad the country is a featureless, dead flat plain. The only cover from fire is afforded by the irrigation channels leading out of the River Tigris at intervals of roughly half a mile. Cover from view is afforded by a belt of tamarisk extending along the river banks for a breadth of about two hundred yards on each side. It should be borne in mind, however, that this is only generally true, since in places there may be no vegetation whatsoever, while in more favoured localities this belt of tamarisk extends inland for as much as half a mile.

The Action at Shaikh Saad, January 7th, 1916.

The Brigade was soon advancing towards the sound of the guns. After an hour's march Commanding Officers were summoned by the Brigade Commander, by whom the situation was, as far as possible, explained, and orders for an attack issued. The Brigade was to attack with two battalions, the other two being in support. The 9th Bhopal Infantry was to be a supporting battalion, in echelon on the right. The enemy were said to be holding a position covering Shaikh Saad, but we were without maps and the information received was exceedingly scanty. After a brief time to allow of orders reaching the troops the Brigade moved off half right from its original direction of march, battalions moving into their allotted positions in artillery formation.

A few shells were bursting high in the air and occasionally bursts of fairly distant musketry were heard. At a rough guess, the Battalion was still some two miles from the nearest enemy when a shell burst in the middle of the machine gun section. Lieutenant Cameron Ker, Battalion Machine Gun Officer, and a number of machine gunners were wounded. "A" and "C" Companies, who were leading, at once extended and promptly came under very heavy rifle fire. This was directed, not at them, but at the 6th Jats, who were in front. No enemy was visible, however, and the Battalion continued to advance. All companies were now extended and were gradually closing up to the 6th Jats. Suddenly the Brigadier appeared and shouted to the Commanding Officer, " The enemy are advancing over there " (pointing to the Battalion's right flank). " Move the 9th Bhopals towards him and stop him with the bayonet if necessary."

All four companies at once wheeled and moved off at the double in the new direction. At first they were subjected to a galling enfilade fire ; but this, and the casualties it had caused, were soon left behind. The Battalion's new direction appeared to be taking it away from the action altogether, and, after having moved nearly a mile, as no enemy could be seen, the Battalion halted. " A," " B " and " C " Companies, occupying a frontage of about one thousand yards, were in the front line, while " D " Company was in support.

It was now about noon, and the Battalion was ordered to dig in to meet the expected attack. By nightfall the Battalion was solidly entrenched, but the expected attack did not take place. During the night enterprising enemy patrols attempted to approach the Battalion's position, but were promptly driven off. Apart from this, the night and the following day passed uneventfully. After sunset on the 8th the Battalion was withdrawn somewhat to its left rear and given another position in which to entrench. This was because the 35th Brigade on the left had been withdrawn, and the front was now to be occupied by the 19th and 21st Brigades only.

This, the Battalion's first action in Mesopotamia, was a most unsatisfactory one from its own point of view. It had seen no sign of the enemy and did not appear to have achieved anything, yet had suffered 87 casualties. While entrenching this second position, the Battalion was subjected to a certain amount of desultory fire which gradually died down until, about midnight, it ceased altogether. Next morning, the 9th, the whole force advanced on Shaikh Saad, which it reached without opposition at about 4 p.m. The enemy had retired to a position about Orah, with the River Wadi between him and us on the left bank.

The whole force was in an exhausted condition by the time it reached Shaikh Saad, and it was decided to halt next day. Air reports and cavalry reconnaissances indicated that the bulk of the enemy had retired to the Es Sinn position, leaving a small force near Orah. By the 11th, however, the enemy had once more advanced and was now in position along the Wadi. To induce the enemy to assume that the British force intended to halt, the 7th Division was ordered to dig a position covering Shaikh Saad along the left bank, while the troops under General Kemball on the right bank were to prolong the position on that side. For this purpose, at 7 p.m., January 11th, the 21st Brigade advanced northwards for about three miles. Here it extended, took up a position about two miles long, and at once commenced to dig in. This position was occupied all next day.

Meanwhile General Aylmer was completing his plans for an assault on the Wadi position on the following day. The general idea was to pin the enemy to his trenches along the Wadi with the 28th Brigade, whilst the 7th Division moved round his left flank and eventually surrounded him. At 6.15 p.m. on the 12th, in order to carry out the above operation, the 7th Division and the 6th Cavalry Brigade concentrated on the right of the position already entrenched. A difficult night march followed, and at about 2.30 a.m. the 7th Division and the 6th Cavalry Brigade were ordered to halt and to await dawn. The 7th Division was formed up at the position of assembly in line of brigades, in the order 21st, 19th, 35th from left to right. Owing to a thick mist at dawn, however, no forward movement was made by the 7th Division for a time. But at 7.30 a.m. on the 13th the 21st Brigade advanced, while the 19th and 35th Brigades conformed to their movement, advancing in echelon on their right.

The Action of the Wadi, January 13th, 1916.

The 21st Brigade, who had been strengthened by the addition of the 6th Jats, advanced with that unit on the right, with the Black Watch, the 41st Dogras, the 9th Bhopal Infantry, and the 9th Gurkhas, in that order on its left. Each battalion had one company in the firing line. The leading troops crossed the Wadi soon after starting without difficulty, but the artillery and wheeled transport were unable to negotiate its steep banks. Half a mile beyond the Wadi the leading companies came under heavy fire from an enemy so well concealed that nothing could be seen of him.

Landmarks that would have helped, and precise information as to the enemy's position, were entirely lacking. In spite of this, "B" Company, which was leading the

Battalion, succeeded in getting to within two hundred yards of the enemy before they were finally checked. The 9th Gurkhas had inclined to the left, and a gap, which gradually widened, appeared between them and "B" Company. This gap "C" Company Commander decided to fill.

Shortly afterwards Lieutenant-Colonel Thomas, the Battalion Commander, came up from the rear, confirmed the Company Commander's decision, and then went forward himself to "B" Company. On arriving in line with "B" Company, "C" Company also was held up. All this time fire from the enemy had been very heavy and well directed, causing severe losses. No effective reply was possible, as no target whatsoever was to be seen.

By 10 a.m. the brigade attack had come to a standstill, and the leading troops were busy with their "Sirhind" entrenching tools constructing such cover as was possible against the enemy's galling fire. After nightfall picks and shovels were brought up and effective cover was completed. In the early afternoon ammunition with the forward troops was getting low. Many attempts to replenish it were made, but with one exception not a single carrier got through. Any movement in the leading lines was at once followed by a fresh outburst of fire from the enemy, and eventually any attempt to bring up ammunition had to be abandoned until it could be done under cover of darkness.

During the following night the enemy maintained a fairly heavy fire, but this gradually diminished and finally ceased. At about 4 p.m. patrols found that he had retired. When the Turk intends to retire and has not actually been driven out at the point of the bayonet, he invariably adopts this method, which, in point of fact, in Southern Mesopotamia is the only feasible plan.

Casualties.

The Battalion's casualties during this action were Lieutenant-Colonel Thomas, Major Jamieson and Lieutenant Roberts wounded, of whom the two former subsequently died. Three Indian officers were wounded, 7 Indian other ranks killed and 84 wounded. Practically all the casualties occurred in "B" and "C" Companies. "A" Company, who had been detailed to help the Pioneers in making ramps to enable the guns to cross the Wadi, and subsequently to act as escort to the guns, and "D" Company, who were in support, hardly came under fire.

January 13th, 1916, is a memorable day for the Battalion, in that it brought us that most coveted of all decorations, the Victoria Cross. The circumstances in which it was earned are as follows:—After leaving "C" Company Commander Lieutenant-Colonel Thomas, as already mentioned, went forward towards "B" Company. At this time the enemy fire had increased in intensity in order to prevent "C" Company's forward movement to fill the gap on the left of "B" Company. When about forty yards from "B" Company, Lieutenant-Colonel Thomas was shot down. Seeing his Commanding Officer lying wounded, Sepoy Chatta Singh rushed forward and bandaged the wound.

Victoria Cross earned by Sepoy Chatta Singh.

The spot where Colonel Thomas fell was bare and as flat as a billiard table. Less than two hundred yards away the enemy continued to direct a heavy fire towards them. After bandaging Colonel Thomas's wound, Chatta Singh heroically placed himself in such a position that his body acted as a shield to his Commanding Officer.

In this position the gallant sepoy dug with his entrenching tool for some hours, and slowly but surely constructed a bullet-proof cover for them both. Colonel Thomas's left leg was shattered half-way between the knee and the ankle, and he suffered such agony that at times the pain drew from him groans that could be heard by his men during lulls in the fighting. Chatta Singh's efforts to comfort and reassure his Commanding Officer could also be heard. Further aid was impossible before nightfall, for any attempt to carry Colonel Thomas to safety during daylight would have meant destruction of the whole party. When eventually Colonel Thomas was rescued he was nearly delirious through pain and loss of blood, but, in spite of this, he did not forget to impress on his rescuers the great and unselfish gallantry of Chatta Singh. The honour which came to Sepoy Chatta Singh, and through him to the Battalion, was thoroughly well earned, and is one of which the Battalion will always be proud.

January 14th was a quiet day, and the 21st Brigade closed in on the 41st Dogras and advanced as far as the river bank, where it bivouacked. The weather turned wet again, and for the next three days conditions were about as miserable as they could be. The enemy had, meanwhile,

MAP NO. 4

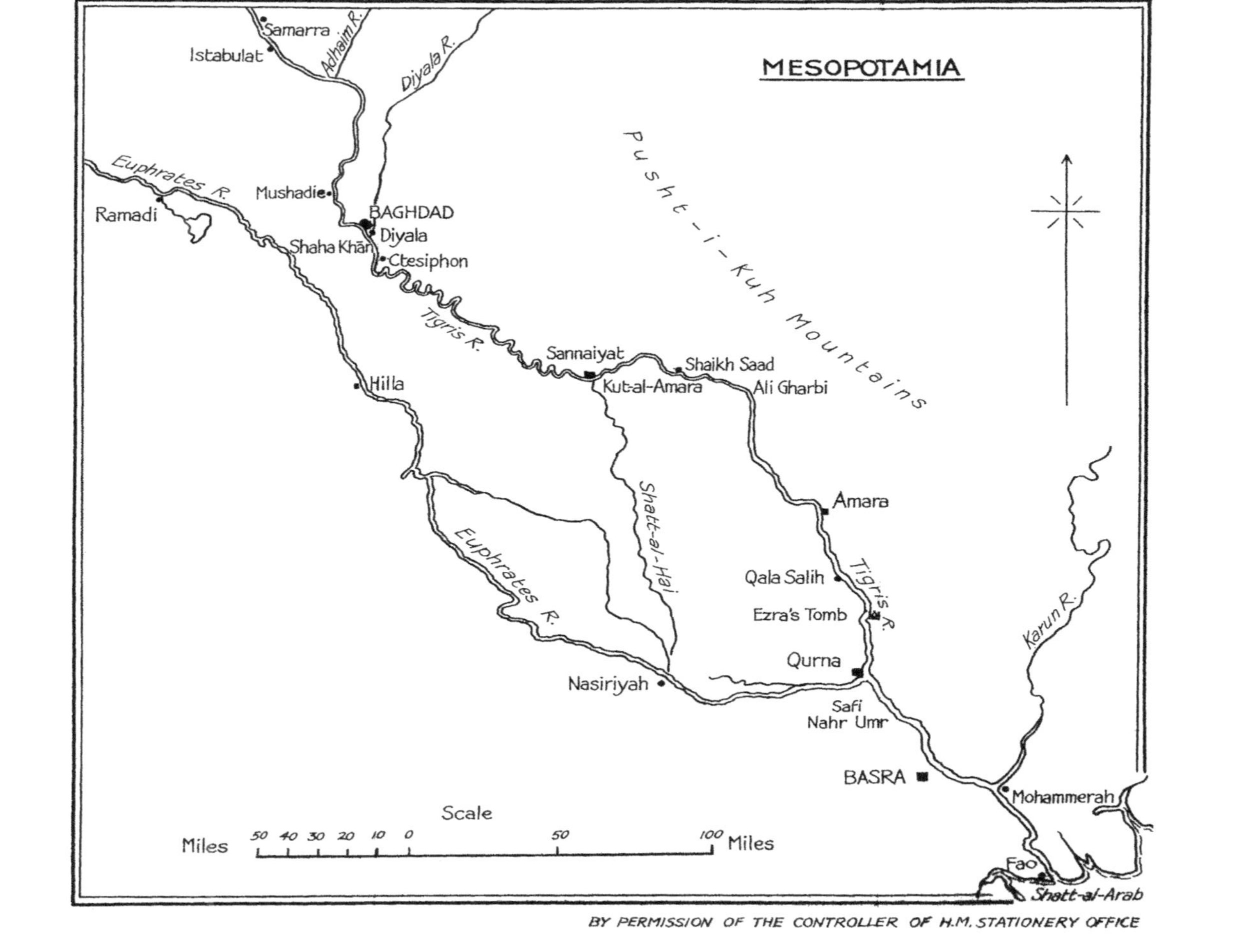

BY PERMISSION OF THE CONTROLLER OF H.M. STATIONERY OFFICE

retired to a previously entrenched position about three-quarters of a mile in extent, with his right flank on the river and his left flank on a marsh. This was, later on, known as the Hannah position, and was situated about two miles upstream of our bivouac of the 14th. The original intention was to attack this position on the morning of the 14th, and then the 7th Division was actually advancing to do so when Corps Headquarters postponed the attack to ensure adequate artillery preparation from both banks of the river. Owing largely to bad weather and mud, the attack was postponed from day to day; by the 19th, however, preparations were complete, and the assault was fixed for January 21st.

Meanwhile, on January 19th the 21st Brigade was temporarily broken up. The Battalion was attached to the 19th Brigade and the other battalions to the 35th Brigade. The Battalion was detailed as Brigade reserve, and so remained until the evening of the 20th.

CHAPTER XV

(See Map facing page 106.)

Preparations for the Attack on the Hannah position.

As already stated, the weather conditions caused the postponement of the attack from day to day. Of the time thus allowed him the enemy made the fullest use. He strengthened his front by means of wire entanglements, and threw up adequate cover against enfilade fire from the right bank. Meanwhile, on the 14th, the concentration of the 3rd Division had been completed, and the relieving force now consisted of the 3rd and 7th Divisions and Corps troops. General Aylmer himself considered it impossible to take Hannah without losing half his force. He considered his only plan was to advance on both banks, but feared this would be very slow.

The 19th and 35th Brigades had been entrenching towards the Hannah position since the 14th instant. When the Battalion joined the 19th Brigade, which was on the right, their front trench was about 400 yards distant from the enemy. At this time, however, the trench system was not continuous, and there were practically no communication trenches.

On the 20th the Battalion received orders to relieve the 92nd Punjabis in the front line. The Battalion set out as soon as it was dark, but as there were no communication trenches in this sector it lost two Indian officers and twenty Indian other ranks before reaching the 92nd Punjabis. On completing the relief, "A" and "B" Companies were at once sent forward about 200 yards to prepare and occupy a new position; "C" Company meanwhile occupying the original front line and "D" Company, in reserve, a trench to the rear. During the 20th and the night 20th-21st our artillery carried out bombardments, and the 35th Brigade advanced their leading lines to within 300 yards of the enemy.

First Attack on Hannah.

The orders for January 21st were for the 35th Brigade, supported by the 9th Brigade, to assault the enemy's right, while the 19th Brigade was to hold his left and, when opportunity arose, to close with him

The battle began at 7.45 a.m. by a ten minute artillery

bombardment. Some of the assaulting troops of the 35th Brigade reached the enemy position and occupied portions of it for a short time. But the enemy fire was so severe that only a handful of the supporters got forward. Of the supporting Brigade, the 9th, portions only of one unit reached the enemy trenches, the remainder being definitely held up in our own front line. The enemy then launched a counter-attack against the captured portion of his position, and by midday had regained it.

During this time there was no movement along the front of the 19th Brigade. As soon as the 35th Brigade began its assault, gun and rifle fire was directed at it from the whole enemy line. Against the left of the 35th Brigade it did little or no damage beyond severing all telephonic communication between units and Brigade Headquarters and frustrating every attempt to restore it. In the 19th Brigade units were in disconnected trenches, battalions being cut off from one another and from intercommunication even with their own companies. At about 9 a.m. the supporting battalions of the 19th Brigade advanced, but only a handful of men, without officers or non-commissioned officers, and in a state of confusion, reached the Battalion's support trench.

At about 1 p.m. the 28th Brigade was ordered to assault in conjunction with the 19th Brigade, but only a few isolated men succeeded in advancing as far as the Battalion's Headquarters, and they, like those of the 19th Brigade earlier in the day, had no news to impart. During this advance the enemy fire was exceptionally heavy and well controlled. The moment a line of men rose to advance it was subjected to a hail of fire; as soon as this line lay down, the fire instantly ceased. This continued throughout that day, and says much for the training and discipline of the enemy opposed to us. It was not until dusk that the Battalion learnt that the two advances already described were intended to be serious assaults on the enemy position.

Failure of the Attack.

Meanwhile, it had become evident to Divisional Headquarters that the attack could be pressed no more that day, and orders were therefore issued for units to disengage and withdraw to the trenches occupied prior to the bombardment of the 20th. To add to the confusion, rain had begun to fall at noon, and by nightfall many of the men were so numbed with cold as to be practically helpless. While withdrawing, units had been ordered to clear the battlefield of casualties, but the condition of the men and the darkness of the night were such that this task was not completed until midnight. When finally the Battalion had arrived at the reserve trenches of the 19th and 20th, these were found to be little better than holes, full of water. The Battalion's casualties this day, including those which occurred during the relief of the 92nd Punjabis, were three Indian officers and 61 Indian other ranks. The available rifles of the Battalion were now only about two hundred. So depleted had the Battalion become that it was considered advisable to re-form it into two composite companies by combining the remnants of "C" with "A" and "D" with "B" Company.

Conditions in Mesopotamia.

Next day the Battalion rejoined the 21st Brigade and enjoyed two days of comparative comfort—that is to say, it had tents to keep off the wind and rain, but the ground on which tents were pitched was literally a quagmire. It may not be out of place to relate a few incidents to show the general discomfort at this time. Shortage of transport limited fuel to bare cooking requirements, so none was available to dry clothing and consequently everyone was continually wet and cold. Field Ambulances had no staff to attend to their patients, and units had therefore to provide orderlies to cook for and look after their own sick and wounded. This entailed great hardships on patients since units had no cooks to spare, and trained hospital orderlies among the rank and file were practically non-existent. Instances occurred of men leaving hospital and rejoining their Battalion although still suffering from dysentery, fever or other troubles. One Indian officer who did this and was asked his reason replied, "Sahib, with the Regiment I have a chance, but in hospital I should certainly die."

Divisional Routine Order No. 401 of March 24th, 1916, reads: "When officers are admitted to Field Ambulance they should, if possible, take their own tents, cup, plate, knife, fork, etc., with them." All the extra issue of rations, such as sugar, milk, tea, etc., so necessary for Indian troops, were absolutely unobtainable. One more incident to illustrate how rain and the consequent mud hampered movement. One night the Battalion had to move to the river bank, two hundred yards distant from camp. On arriving at the bank it was discovered that a certain number (including a

British Officer) had lost their boots. The mud, into which they sank nearly knee deep, had pulled them off!

After the failure of the attack on Hannah on the 21st, it was recognized that, in view of the state of the troops and the weather, a further assault next day was out of the question, and that a breathing space was necessary. On being informed of this, General Townshend commandeered all food supplies in Kut, rationed the local inhabitants, and reported that on reduced rations he could hold out till April 17th. Reinforcements for the relief force were on the way, including the 13th Division recently evacuated from Gallipoli. And steps were also taken to ensure if possible success at the next attempt. On January 26th General Townshend reported that a Turkish Division had crossed the Hai. To meet what appeared to be an enemy counter-offensive down the right bank, General Aylmer ferried across a large part of the force from the left bank. The Battalion, together with the rest of the 21st Brigade, took part in this movement. The Battalion remained on the right bank until February 5th, going out on two occasions in support of cavalry reconnaissances. The enemy counter-offensive did not materialize nor was the reported division ever traced. It has been suggested the report was based on a fallacy due to mirage.

Trench Warfare.

On return to the left bank the Battalion received a much-needed reinforcement, consisting of two Indian officers and 141 men of the 7th Rajputs. Next day there arrived from the same regiment a further draft, consisting of two British officers (Lieutenant Tyndall, 7th Rajputs, and Lieutenant Newman, I.A.R.O.), one Indian officer and 37 men. Both these drafts were kept together and were formed into new "C" and "D" Companies respectively. By February 8th a regular system of trench warfare had been organized. On this date the 21st Brigade relieved the 28th Brigade, the Battalion relieving the 62nd Punjabis. The Battalion was disposed with—"A" Company in the front line, "B" Company in support, and "C" and "D" Companies in reserve.

In addition a picquet of one British officer and 25 rifles were entrenched about two hundred yards in advance of our front line, to which it was subsequently linked by a communication trench. Three days later a fresh picquet post was constructed one hundred and thirty yards forward, and again similarly linked up with the trench. This was followed by making a new front line by means of joining up all advanced picquet posts. During the execution of this work the enemy kept up desultory fire, which caused comparatively few casualties, the Battalion's amounting to five men wounded. Throughout this time the weather continued wet and cold, and the troops, who were still clad in khaki drill and without shelter, suffered much hardship and discomfort. On February 18th the Battalion was relieved by a battalion of the 19th Brigade, and went into camp at Orah.

Demonstration in the Suwaikiyeh Marsh.

In the middle of February General Aylmer decided to make a surprise demonstration against the rear of the enemy's position at Hannah. His object, as announced to the troops, was to inflict as much damage as possible on the enemy in their main camp behind Hannah and force him to disclose his dispositions. General Aylmer considered it even possible that the enemy might be induced to vacate his position, in which case he would follow him up. General Townshend might thus get an opportunity for offensive measures, for which he was to be prepared. Originally planned for the night of 20th-21st, rain caused the project to be postponed for twenty-four hours. Here, in order to get a clear grasp of the operation as a whole, it may be well to relate the movements of the force to which the Battalion belonged.

On the night 21st-22nd February, General Gorringe, with the Cavalry Brigade, 3rd Division plus 36th Brigade, 28th Battery R.F.A., and 23rd Mountain Battery, moved up the right bank. At daybreak his guns bombarded the enemy's camp near the Fallahiyah bend, causing considerable confusion. Part of his column moved upstream to a point opposite Sannaiyat. Here the right bank commands the left, and the river was low and the current slack. In his report, General Gorringe says that, had he been in possession of a pontoon train, he could, by taking advantage of the surprise he had effected, have crossed the river and hemmed the Turks into their Hannah position.

On February 21st intimation was received that the 21st Brigade was to take part in certain operations starting that night. It was to appear on the enemy left flank on the morning of the 22nd and make him believe an attack was to be pushed home from this side. The guns which were to accompany the Brigade were meanwhile to shell the enemy camps. The Brigade and attached artillery left Orah at 1 a.m. on the 22nd, the Battalion leading the column.

The night was fine with a three-quarter moon, so the march presented no difficulty. At 4.30 a.m. the Column was halted, took up a position with battalions in line and awaited dawn. When daylight came the Column found itself with the Suwaikiyeh Marsh in front and on its right, and the enemy about 2,000 yards away on the further side of it. At 7.45 a.m. " C " and " D " Companies advanced in line about 500 yards to the edge of the marsh. The enemy at once opened fire with guns of small calibre, familiarly known as " pip-squeaks," and inflicted four slight casualties. On arriving at the edge of the marsh, the two companies started to entrench, but soon found they could not dig deeper than eighteen inches, as water was so near the surface; in fact, on the right of this line even a trench six inches deep filled with water in an hour. The day passed quietly. During the night 23rd-24th Lieutenant Tyndall and twelve men reconnoitred the ground towards the enemy to find out whether it was favourable for the movement of troops and reported it to be so.

During the next two days the Brigade set to work to construct a trench system. The enemy on his side of the marsh also was similarly busy and was beginning to find our range with machine-gun and rifle fire. At 1 a.m. on the 26th entrenching ceased. Each unit then left a few men in its sector of the front trench, and by 5.30 a.m. assembled the remainder in rear of the position. The object was to mislead the enemy to believe we were sending up reinforcements. At dawn the troops assembled in rear of the position advanced towards the trenches. The enemy fired a few shells, but these did no damage. By noon units were quietly withdrawn to the rear and right of the trenches for the purpose of carrying out another manœuvre by which it was hoped that the enemy might be induced to man his newly-constructed lines thickly and so offer our guns a good target.

This time the Brigade was formed up in lines of half battalions at three hundred yards distance. Each line consisted of eight platoons in column of fours at one hundred yards interval. The 9th Bhopal Infantry led the Brigade, with their leading platoons pushing along some dummy pontoons which had been received earlier in the day. The Battalion's orders were to proceed towards the enemy trenches for half an hour after entering the water of the marsh and then return to their starting-point.

On its north shore the marsh shelved very gradually, and at the end of the half hour's advance the troops were still only knee deep and had a good firm bottom all the way. What effect this manœuvre had on the enemy is not known, but he did not open fire. Either he was waiting for the advancing troops to get nearer and into deeper water, when he could have them at his mercy, or else mirage hid the movement altogether. When, however, the troops were half-way on their return journey, the enemy opened artillery fire ; but his ranging was faulty and there were no casualties. Meanwhile every available gun of ours on both banks of the river was heavily shelling the enemy's new trenches. By 4 p.m. the troops were back at the starting-point, and by 11.40 p.m. the Brigade was in camp at Orah, where it spent the following night before relieving the 28th Brigade in the trenches.

Duties in the Trenches.

Communications had by now been so improved that the Battalion which was detailed as Brigade reserve was able to carry out the relief by day. The Battalion's duties in this area consisted chiefly in clearing trenches of mud and digging new communications. On March 4th the Battalion relieved two of the units in the forward trenches. By this time the front line had been carried so much nearer the enemy that the reserve battalion was now in the trench which had previously been the front line.

Gas Alarms.

It was now rumoured that the enemy contemplated using gas. On March 7th gas masks and gongs to sound the alarm were issued. On more than one occasion various units had reported that a smell of gas had been wafted over from the enemy. One evening while the Brigadier was going round our front he suddenly stopped, turned to the Battalion Commander, and declared that he could smell gas. As the latter had not been in France, he could only note the aroma for a future occasion. Later, when the Hannah position had been assaulted and occupied, the Battalion Commander encountered a scent by now familiar. A short investigation brought to light the gas manufactory—namely, a few unburied Turks who had been thrown over the parados of the trenches

Dujailah Redoubt.

By early March the relieving force was stronger by three Brigades and some artillery, and a territorial division, from Egypt, was well on the way. General Aylmer decided that the time had come to resume the advance on Kut. For this purpose he decided to leave a weak force in front of Hannah trenches while attacking with all available strength the enemy in their position at Dujailah and Es Sinn. The operation had originally been fixed for March 6th, but had twice to be postponed on account of rain.

On March 6th, 7th and 8th a series of artillery bombardments, accompanied by intensive small arm fire, were carried out both by day and by night with the object of inducing the enemy to believe an assault was intended and to divert his attention from the main issue. When these bombardments took place by day the enemy sat tight, but at night his rifle and machine-gun fire was quite as spirited as ours. On March 7th the attack on the Dujailah was made, but ended in failure, and the force was withdrawn. On the 11th the Battalion went into Brigade reserve, spending the rest of this tour of duty carrying up *chevaux-de-frise* and sapping boards to the front line, and in clearing and levelling communications. On March 14th the 21st Brigade were withdrawn from the trenches for a week, returning on the 21st.

After the failure at Dujailah it was decided that no further advance should be made until the three infantry brigades and if possible one of the artillery brigades of the 13th Division had arrived at the front. In these circumstances the sappers and miners and pioneers were set to work sapping as far forward as possible. On the 21st, when the 21st Brigade returned to the trenches, our front line was about three hundred yards from the enemy. By the 30th two new front lines had been constructed, the last being just one hundred yards from the enemy. The 13th Division also had concentrated by March 24th at Shaikh Saad.

CHAPTER XVI.

By March 30th the 3rd Division had advanced along the right bank, and its forward positions were about the line Mason's Mounds—Thorny Nullah. The intention now was to work up the left bank, capture Hannah, then entrench a position along a north to south line from Suwaikiyah Marsh to the northern extremity of the Fallahiyah bend preparatory to attacking the next enemy position at Sannaiyat. On the 30th and 31st our artillery did a lot of wire-cutting and appeared to do considerable damage to the enemy front trench. The 13th Division was detailed to capture Hannah and was to have relieved the 7th Division in the trenches on April 1st. But heavy rain came on early in the day and the assault had to be postponed. The relief was actually carried out at 3 p.m. on April 2nd, and the Battalion was accommodated in the tents of the 133rd Indian Field Ambulance. At 8 p.m. on April 4th the 7th Division again moved into the trenches to be ready to support the 13th Division when it assaulted next morning. The 21st Brigade led, and occupied Manchester Trench. On the following morning at 4.55 a.m. the 13th Division assaulted. The enemy had evacuated his position the previous night, leaving only a few snipers who at first inflicted a few casualties but were soon either killed or captured.

Second Attack on Hannah.

During the assault the 7th Division were in support of the 13th Division, the 9th Bhopal Infantry leading the Division. A short halt was made in the enemy front trench, and, at the head of one of his communication trenches, the following notice which now hangs in the Officers' Mess of the Regiment, was found :—

"Au revoir. Nous vous reverrons sur le prochain champs de battaille.—Nahiol."

The 13th Division continued to advance until held up during the afternoon in front of the Fallahiyah position. After an artillery bombardment at 7.45 p.m., the enemy's position was rushed and the 21st Brigade ordered forward to take over from the leading brigade of the 13th Division.

Capture of Fallahiyah.

The Battalion relieved the 9th Warwicks, taking over a

line extending from the river for about 300 yards to the north. Patrols were at once sent forward, but found no sign of the enemy. Meanwhile, the other two brigades of the 7th Division were concentrating behind the 21st Brigade to carry out an assault at dawn on the 6th against Sannaiyat. To reach the enemy before dawn these two brigades had to traverse a distance of some three miles. The intervening ground proved to be very cut up with trenches, and, to add to the difficulty, the night was very dark. As a result the columns were considerably delayed, and, when dawn broke, the foremost troops found themselves still some two thousand yards short of the enemy position. The Turks were evidently fully prepared to meet an attack, for, at 5.30 a.m. a heavy rifle and machine-gun fire came from their trenches and was followed immediately by gun fire from both banks of the river. The 28th Brigade, who were leading, pressed gallantly on to within five hundred yards of the enemy, where they were finally held up. The 19th Brigade, who were in support, were held up about one thousand yards from the enemy's position and no further advance was made that day.

First Attack on Sannaiyat.

At 6.30 a.m. the 21st Brigade which, at dawn had come into Divisional reserve, was ordered to advance and support the attack of the two leading brigades. This order appears to have been somewhat premature, for soon after the Brigade was halted for the remainder of the day. During the morning Lieutenant Morrison and a certain number of men were wounded by our own artillery then handicapped by prematures, due to defective ammunition.

About midday the misfortunes of the 28th Brigade were added to by a strong " shamal " (north wind). This drove the waters of the Suwaikiyeh Marsh towards the river, flooding this area and drowning a number of the wounded of this brigade. The 28th Brigade's front lines were subsequently flooded and they were forced to retire.

Owing to the water of the Tigris being in flood at this season of the year, the capture of Sannaiyat was believed to be the only way of getting through to Kut. The 7th Division was therefore ordered to advance on the morning of the 7th with the object of gaining as much ground as possible preparatory to making another assault during the ensuing night. The

Second Attack on Sannaiyat.

19th and 28th Brigades advanced according to plan, supported by the 21st Brigade. Before the leading troops had got within assaulting distance, however, they were brought to a standstill by enemy fire. During the night the 7th Division gained another 300 yards and there entrenched.

Third Attack on Sannaiyat.

On the 9th, at dawn, the 13th Division delivered an unsuccessful attack against the enemy. The 7th Division was to have supported this attack, but was not required. Next day the 21st Brigade relieved the 28th Brigade in the trenches. The Battalion was on the right of the line adjoining the Suwaikiyeh Marsh.

Early on April 12th a "shamal" started, and by 4.30 p.m. the waters of the marsh burst into the trenches and carried away the parapets. Trenches and communications were barricaded against the water, but these in turn were washed away, and by 5 p.m. the Battalion's trenches were under water. The Battalion was therefore ordered to leave its trenches and withdraw. The enemy who knew the ranges exactly, made full use of this opportunity, and in a very short time had inflicted twenty casualties amongst the retiring groups. It was therefore deemed advisable to discontinue the movement until dark. The men were made to lie down in the water behind any cover available, and as the water did not rise more than six inches above ground level so they were able to remain where they were and retire after dark at their leisure. About half a mile in rear the Battalion reached dry land and were ordered to entrench again. Here it remained for the next few days, with all ranks busily employed strengthening bunds, etc., against another flood. On the 17th the Battalion was back in its old trenches and continued to work at anti-flood measures. But all in vain, for on the 19th another "shamal" once more caused the trenches to be flooded, and they had again to be evacuated. The Battalion was withdrawn some thousand yards and occupied an old Turkish trench.

Meanwhile, the position in Kut was becoming serious. General Townshend reported that, after the 23rd, with the exception of meat, his troops would have to depend entirely on such supplies as aeroplanes could drop him, and he gave April 29th as the extreme date to which he could hold out. On the right bank the 3rd and 13th Divisions had advanced as far as Beit Aiessa, but were here definitely held up, and the only chance of effecting the relief of Kut in time appeared to lie in the capture of the Sannaiyat position by direct assault.

Fourth Attack on Sannaiyat.

Though the marsh had not succeeded in dislodging us till the 19th, it had come in between us and the Turks, and by the 17th there was a continuous sheet of water about 100 yards wide between the trench systems. Next night patrols working through this water found a strip 600 yards wide about the centre, where the water was only a few inches deep, except for shell-holes, and over which an advance would be less difficult than through the deeper water and more slippery mud to the north and south. An attack on a two-brigade front across this strip was accordingly decided on for the 20th, but the " shamal " of the 19th again postponed matters. On the 21st, therefore, orders were issued for this attack next day, with the 21st Brigade on the right and the 19th Brigade on the left. At 8 p.m. on the 21st the 21st Brigade formed up in the following order :—The Composite British Battalion (a battalion composed of drafts intended for the Norfolks and Dorsets, who were in Kut, and called the " Norsets "), 9th Bhopals, 6th Jats, 1/8th Gurkhas.

Patrols during the night reported that the level of the water in the marsh and in the river had risen, and that there was now only a narrow strip of dry land some one hundred and fifty yards wide leading from our trenches to those of the enemy. Accordingly, the plan of attack had to be altered. The new orders reached the troops concerned only half an hour before zero hour. The 19th Brigade were to lead the attack, followed by the 28th and 21st Brigades in that order. As the frontage of the attack was limited to one hundred and fifty yards, battalions were to advance in lines of companies at fifty paces interval.

The attack was launched at 7.30 a.m., some two hours after dawn. From the moment they left their trenches the attackers were subjected to a very accurate and well-controlled fire. The Turkish position was a mile wide, and, as the frontage of the attack was only one hundred and fifty yards, the Turks were able to direct converging machine-gun and rifle fire on the attackers. In spite of heavy losses the 19th Brigade reached the Turkish front line only to find it unoccupied and full of water. The trench was too wide for the troops to jump over and they were therefore forced to scramble through as best they could. In doing this, their rifles became clogged with mud, and some confusion was inevitable. In spite of this the leading troops struggled gallantly on.

The 19th Brigade succeeded in entering the Turkish second line. This was found to be only lightly held, and when victory seemed within our grasp the enemy delivered a well-timed counter-attack against our right. With their rifles clogged with mud, as already mentioned, from scrambling through water-logged trenches and shell-holes, our troops were unable to use them with much effect against the counter-attacking enemy and, in spite of prompt support by our artillery and machine guns from the right bank of the river the enemy's counter-attack was completely successful. By 8.30 a.m. the few survivors of these two brigades were back in their original trenches. In this battle the 9th Bhopal Infantry were not engaged; the battalion in front of them, the "Norsets," had just left their trenches preparatory to advancing, when orders were received that no more troops were to attack. At 10 a.m. the Turks showed a flag of truce which we reciprocated. An armistice was arranged lasting till 3 p.m., during which time the 7th Division was allowed to remove its wounded lying more than three hundred yards from the Turkish trenches.

That night the following telegram was sent to India by General Lake :—

". . . Gorringe considers that the troops have, for the present, reached the limit of their offensive powers, and that they are not capable of further effort without two or three days' rest. They have been engaged continuously since April 5th, fighting the enemy and floods, and have in this period suffered 9,700 casualties, which represents twenty-five per cent. of his fighting force. We are still twelve miles from Kut on the right bank and fifteen miles on the left bank. Floods on either flank limit our power of manœuvre, and each attack, without several days of artillery preparation, which our time-limit precludes, is costly . . ."

Thus ended all efforts to relieve Kut which surrendered on April 29th and also all attacks against Sannaiyat for some months.

On the 24th the 21st Brigade moved across to the right bank of the Tigris and took up a position near Abu Roman mounds in support of the 3rd Division which was operating in the vicinity of Chahela. The Battalion remained there until the 26th, when it was withdrawn into camp at Thorny Nullah. The weather was now warming up, flies were increasing at an alarming rate and cholera had broken out in the Brigade. Flies were a real scourge at this time. It was quite a common sight to see a plate of food so covered with them that the food was literally invisible. Those officers who had their own mosquito net were lucky in that they could eat in comparative comfort, though even a net could not prevent a large number entering whilst food was being handed in. Almost indistinguishable from the ordinary fly was another variety which, armed like a mosquito, punctured the knees and ankles to one's extreme discomfort.

Discomforts of the Hot Weather.

The sandfly had also begun his unwelcome attentions. Darkness brought relief from flies for a few hours, but in their place appeared swarms of sandflies, which kept everyone painfully reminded of their presence. Their bites were most unpleasant and irritating and eventually brought on a seven-day attack of fever, accompanied by severe headache and aching bones. Fortunately one was seldom the victim of more than one attack.

On May 5th the Battalion received a reinforcement of 2 Indian officers and 211 men, most Gaur Brahmins, a class new to the Battalion. They turned out well and did good service later on. Following this accession of strength, the Battalion was reorganized as follows :—

" A " Company :—

Nos. 1 and 2 Platoons ...	Sikhs.
No. 3 Platoon	Rajputs.

" B " Company :—

Nos. 4 and 5 Platoons ...	Muhammadans.
No. 6 Platoon	Brahmins.

" C " Company :—

Nos. 7 and 8 Platoons ...	Brahmins and Rajputs of 11th Rajputs.

" D " Company :—

Nos. 9, 10 and 11 Platoons	Rajputs of 7th and 8th Rajputs.

Within the next few days two further drafts arrived totalling 185 Rajputs, and the Battalion was then completed up to sixteen platoons.

On May 15th the 21st Brigade took over the Beit Aiessa trenches from the 39th Brigade. The Battalion was subjected to occasional sniping from the left bank, but suffered very little from it. On the morning of the 18th an air reconnaissance reported that the enemy had evacuated Chahela, and that there were no enemy between us and Kut on the right bank. The 3rd Division advanced as far as Es Sinn, where they went into camp for the hot weather.

May, June and July, 1916.

As the 21st Brigade was about midway between the 3rd Division and the Advanced Base, it was kept busy escorting convoys backwards and forwards. The Battalion took its turn at this duty and on numerous road-making and other fatigues. It remained near Beit Aiessa until relieved by the 1/4th Gurkhas on June 15th, when it moved into camp at Abu Roman where most of its time was spent on escort duty.

On June 24th the Brigade once more returned to the left bank and camped around the boat bridge at Arab Village. Here duties mainly consisted in finding outposts for the old Hannah position and in escorting convoys to Orah and back. Duties were heavy for the time of year, and the Brigade was glad when, on July 2nd, it was moved up to the central area about the Fallahiyah bend.

From the middle of April it had been gradually warming up, and, in the Mess tent, by the middle of June, a temperature of 132° F. had been reached. Fortunately nights were cool, and refreshing sleep was possible if due precautions were taken to keep sandflies at bay. Mosquito curtains of the ordinary texture had too large a mesh. A mesh fine enough to keep them out was too stifling for use in such a climate, but citronella or paraffin oil served to keep sandflies at bay as long as the smell remained.

On July 3rd we relieved the 53rd Sikhs without incident. This tour was very quiet as far as enemy activity was concerned. Every morning, with the sun behind us, our guns and snipers made matters unpleasant for the Turks, but in the afternoon with the light behind him the tables were turned. The heat in the trenches was stifling as we were below ground level and so lost the benefit of any air that was moving. Flies swarmed until sundown and were then relieved by sandflies. For protection from the sun large dugouts had been made and roofed over with 160 lb. tents, in these there was at least relief for eyes from the glare. The usual routine now was for each brigade of the Division to have ten days in the trenches and twenty days out.

At this time occurred two incidents worthy of record. The first was the welcome news that leave for a period of one month from date of disembarkation at an Indian port to India was opened to the force. Brevet-Major Jardine, Subedar Rahmat Ali Khan and twenty-two Indian other ranks were at once sent on leave. Many were the hopes entertained of being included in the second and subsequent batches. Alas! Ere the first batch returned all leave was closed in preparation for the operations contemplated for the ensuing cold weather. When the leave draft returned the Battalion discovered it had suffered a great loss. Major Jardine had been ordered to rejoin his own unit. The Battalion thus lost a most efficient officer and cheerful companion, who had been through many trying times with it.

Leave opened.

The other noteworthy incident was the issue to battalions of one telescopic rifle each for the use of snipers. The Battalion was unfortunate, as its rifle was so inaccurate that a marksman could not hit a twelve-inch bull at 100 yards. It received a good one later, but not in time for use during its next spell in the trenches. About this time some officer discovered that a Mills grenade would just fit into an empty enemy shell-case and, with a suitable powder charge, could be projected about 130 yards. The Battalion was given a battery of six of these guns, and these were mounted on the parapet of the front trench and Havildar Sunder Singh (who was appointed Battalion gunner) nightly obtained infinite amusement firing them, being quite convinced that he was causing great havoc amongst the enemy.

On August 12th the Battalion was relieved by the 92nd Punjabis and 125th Rifles. As usual, during a relief the enemy displayed unusual activity with rifle grenades and machine guns. This incident, too, did not at the time receive the consideration it deserved. As, however, subsequent reliefs were always the occasion for an increasingly heavy bombardment, the matter was investigated. Eventually it was assumed that Muhammadan

August, 1916.

deserters to the enemy had given him information by which he worked out the necessary dates. To defeat this, relief dates were made irregular; but the enemy still carried on with his old calendar, and every tenth day those who happened to be in the trenches knew they were in for an extra heavy "strafe."

One day during August the "shamal" began to blow rather stronger than usual, and in twenty-four hours the waters of the Suwaikiyeh Marsh had advanced about half a mile nearer to our camp. When the wind abated and the water began to recede, some of the men of the Battalion who happened to be on the spot noticed many large fish floundering about. The news was quickly passed on, and soon most of the Battalion were on the spot with sticks and sacks. The bag must have been close on one thousand pounds of fish ranging from two to ten pounds. When the water finally receded to its normal limit, the area left dry was covered with tons of dead fish.

By September 3rd our front line was only about one hundred and twenty yards distant from that of the enemy.

September, 1916.

On the night of the 5th our sentries heard a voice from the enemy's trenches calling out in Hindustani. The speaker was endeavouring to convince hearers how much better off he was with the enemy than those of his former comrades who had remained loyal. He concluded his harangue by asking for news of various men of his former company of his regiment.

Next night the deserter was allowed to continue his harangue undisturbed in order to allow a party of British officers to listen to him. He held out various inducements for desertion, and ended up by inviting all men, Muhammadans and Hindus alike, to cross over to the enemy. "Why do you go on serving as sepoys, when you can come over here and become officers and get twenty, thirty or even forty pounds from the Turks." To this, a sepoy of the Battalion, unaware that he was being overheard by a British officer, replied, "Go away and come back and talk to us when you are a General." The following evening when the deserter began Sunder Singh's grenade battery sent a volley of rifle grenades towards him. The deserter's reply was a threat that if we did not stop he would turn his guns on to us. Our second volley must have been more than he bargained for and no more was heard of him that night.

MAP NO. 5

Suwaikiya Marsh
Hannah
Fallahiya
R. Wadi
Wadi Camp
Ora
Arab Village
Mason's Mounds
Thorny Nullah
Sannaiyat
Suwada Marsh
Nukhailat
Croftons Obs. Post
Abu Rumman Mounds
Bait Isa
Chahela Mounds
Twin Pimples
The Narrows
Twin Canals
Shaikh Saad
Sinn Position
Sinn Banks
Sinn Abtar
R. Tigris
Maqasis
Umm al Baram
Shumran
KUT
Dujaila Redoubt
Shatt-al-Hai
Dujaila Depression
Atab
Hai Bridge
MESOPOTAMIA
Map to illustrate operations between
10TH March & 31ST April 1916.
Scale
2 0 2 4 6 8 10 Miles
Turkish positions :-

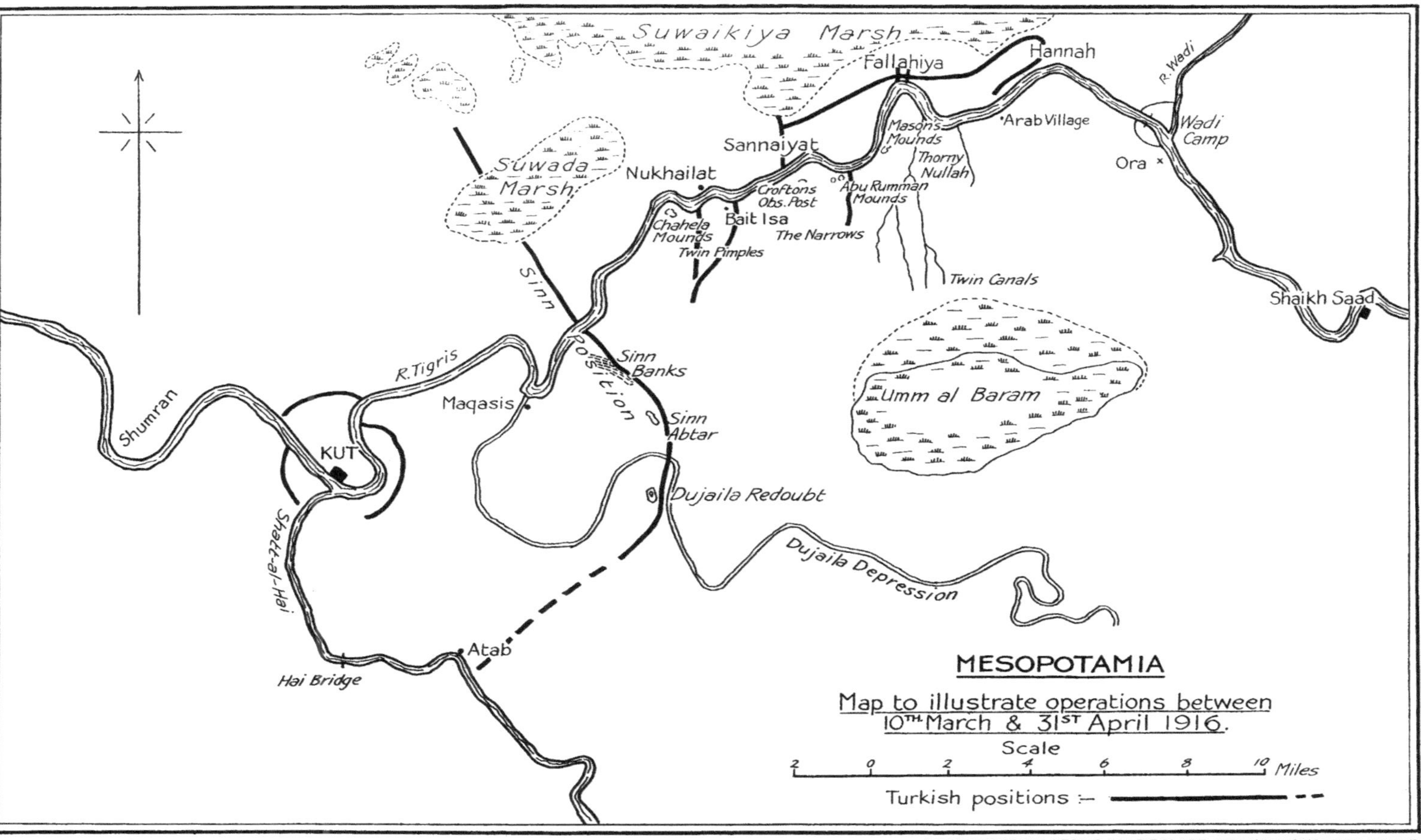

For the next two months there is little to record. As the weather grew cooler, hours of training during the rest periods were gradually increased, and there was marked activity in the trenches in preparation for an offensive which all ranks expected would shortly take place.

While the hot weather brought active operations to a standstill, work from the base upwards continued unceasingly. Transport had been increased by the arrival of various river steamers from India and Burma. A railway was constructed from Qurna to Amara, and an adequate advanced base was formed at Shaikh Saad. All this occupied considerable time as the river level was low, and movement on it greatly impeded by sandbanks. An officer's personal experience will illustrate this. During the July spell out of the trenches he obtained ten days leave to Amara. Seven of these precious days were spent on the journey, mostly stranded on sandbanks. At a later period, when the Inland Water Transport services were organized and functioning properly, this journey averaged forty hours. In spite of all difficulties the work progressed and conditions at the front steadily improved. Serge clothing was issued, rations were sufficient, and, above all, ample reinforcements were made available. In the latter respect the only complaint was the quality of the drafts, a matter over which the supply services had no control.

British Officers.

In July, Captain G. D. Martin joined the staff of the 21st Brigade, and did not rejoin the Battalion until after the Battle of Istabulat, on April 24th, 1917. Major A. de L. Faunce took over command of the Battalion on August 21st from Major H. H. Smith. Major Faunce was not in good health, however, and on October 24th was evacuated sick to India. On October 3rd Lieutenant-Colonel Roosmalecocq, 8th Gurkhas, took over command of the Battalion. His tenure of command was even shorter, as, after one week, he was admitted to hospital, and did not rejoin. Of the remaining officers who arrived with the Battalion in Mesopotamia in December, 1915, Major H. H. Smith, Captain R. d'A. S. Banks, Lieutenant F. C. Roberts and Lieutenant M. Das, I.M.S., were still present.

CHAPTER XVII

THE CAPTURE OF BAGHDAD

General Situation.

DURING the hot weather of 1916 General Maude took over the command of the forces in Mesopotamia. He was always intensely secretive as to his intentions, lest they should come to the knowledge of the Turks. To a regimental officer it was rather an enigma why the force remained inactive after the middle of October, when climatic conditions had become favourable. As for the rank and file, they were convinced that they could drive back the Turks whenever called upon to do so.

The Tigris Force now consisted of a cavalry brigade, four infantry divisions, and adequate complement of artillery. The infantry was organized into two corps, the I Corps consisting of the 3rd and 7th Divisions, the III Corps consisting of the 13th and 14th Divisions.

The situation in December, 1916, was as follows: On the left bank the 7th Division occupied the trenches facing Sannaiyat; on the right bank the other division of the I Corps, the 3rd, held the Sinn Banks and the river from there to near Abu Roman Mounds; the Cavalry and the III Corps were concentrated on the right bank behind the 3rd Division. The enemy held Sannaiyat and a line of trenches along the left bank facing those held by us across the river. On the right bank he occupied a trench system on both banks of the Hai; this system extended back to the Tigris on each side. The road to Baghdad lay along the left bank, but the capture of Sannaiyat would not open it immediately since the Turks had alternative positions in rear which were protected on either flank by river and marsh, as was the case at Sannaiyat, and which would therefore entail costly frontal attacks. General Maude discarded this plan and decided instead to clear the right bank and so be in a position to cross to the left at any point he might select behind Sannaiyat.

Operations on the right bank commenced in the middle of December and did not terminate till February 23rd, 1917, when a successful crossing was made at the Shumran Bend. During the whole of this period the fighting was practically incessant and casualties on both sides severe. The role of the 7th Division was to pin the enemy to Sannaiyat and to assault when opportunity offered.

And now to resume the narrative of the Battalion. On December 5th the Battalion took over the centre section of the Sannaiyat position, the first and second lines each being garrisoned by 160 men, the remainder of the Battalion occupying the third and fourth lines. The events of the next few days are adequately described by the Battalion War Diary. This reads as follows :—

Extracts from War Diary.

" 6/12/16. Very wet day. No tents. Sand bags erected on rest ledges, in rest trenches as walls over which waterproof sheets are spread, thus forming shelter in which men lie. Rest ledges in Prince's Trench finished by pioneers.

" 7/12/16. Visit by G.O.C. 7th Division. Very wet day.

" 8/12/16. Much excitement about three so-called ' strong points ' in enemy line. One appears to have three large apertures or doors facing us, but screened (so that they appear as large as loop-holes) by a high circular parapet some ten to fifteen yards in front. Their purpose unknown.

" 9/12/16. Vermerol sprayers placed in trenches. Coy. Gas N.C.Os. have to test these daily.

" 10/12/16. Left section practised alarm at 5 a.m. Turks took little notice.

" 11/12/16. Rest ledges made in Emperor's Trench and B.O.s' dug-outs commenced in Prince's and Emperor's Trenches.

" 12/12/16. We practised manning trenches 5 a.m., firing two rounds rapid. Enemy work parties dispersed by Lewis guns. Wire cutting by artillery. One N.C.O. and 15 men sent as escort to 9th Brigade Ammunition Column. All kit surplus to move on Transport scale sent back to dumps Four new Lewis guns received.

" 13/12/16. A Turkish deserter stated 7th Regiment of 51st Division on south flank, 9th Regiment of 51st Division and 141st Regiment of 45th Division on north flank, and 142nd Regiment in support at Sannaiyat. No reinforcements expected. Attack by us expected. Observation post at Saffa Mounds reports at 9 a.m. Turks moving from Kut to Sannaiyat. 1.30 to 2.30 p.m. bombardment of enemy front system, repeated at 3.45 to 4.45 p.m. Turkish reply feeble. Patrols sent out at dusk to inspect enemy wire. Enemy found busy repairing trenches after the bombardment.

"14/12/16. 3.30 to 3.40 a.m. bombardment of enemy front system. Little reply from Turks. 6 a.m. to 6.30 a.m. bombardment. 6.30 to 6.32 a.m. an intense bombardment. 6.32 to 6.33½ a.m. barrage lifted to enemy 2nd line. Cat calls by infantry and hoisting of dummies.

"6.33½ a.m. barrage returned to front line and all Stokes mortars fired 5 rounds each. Enemy—all Turks, no Arabs—observed pouring from dug-outs and communications when barrage lifted from 1st line at 6.32 a.m. They held front line strongly. About 50 men got out of their trenches to meet the Black Watch, whom they expected. Their machine guns fired later from a supporting line, but could not be located. Turks took three minutes to man their trenches. On being asked by Brigade all unit commanders said barrage was not effective and an attack would not have succeeded, judging from the ease and rapidity with which Turks manned their front lines and their promptness in opening rifle and machine-gun fire. Bombardment of Sannaiyat 8 a.m. to 9 a.m. Wire was then examined on whole front to report on its condition to 7th Division. Most of the wire was flattened, and much damage done to enemy front line. Russian saps at E8 and E11 restarted towards enemy line. Brigade Commander ordered patrols to go out after dark; if no enemy found, the Brigade was to occupy the first two enemy lines and connect up our trenches with theirs and await orders. Very little warning was given, there were no sandbags and insufficient bombs, little was known of the trenches in front, and the night was very dark. It turned out, however, that Turks were busily repairing their front line. The Turks sent over about thirty big minenwerfer between 11 p.m. and 12 midnight, causing two killed and three wounded in Queen's trench. Our six-inch howitzer silenced the minenwerfer. (Note: It is interesting to know that the minenwerfer now in the Officers' Mess is one of the duds which came over on this occasion.) Our Stokes Mortars fired 330 rounds in retaliation.

"During evening Colonel Wilson, of 1/8th Gurkhas, noticed a bad smell and started a gas scare. This he repeated the following evening. (Note: After the second scare, Major Smith visited the section occupied by the 1/8th Gurkhas out of curiosity. On arrival at the point where the alarm started he was much relieved to come on the familiar scent of Hannah days.)

"15/12/16. Enemy had largely repaired his trenches in the night. Bombardment of positions most of day to cut wire and to fill in the junctions of fire and communication trenches. At 4.8 p.m. practice barrage, 4.9 p.m. lifted to 2nd line, 4.10 p.m. to 4.11 p.m. lifted to 3rd line. Machine guns from Croftons Post fired hard when targets were observed from right bank. Patrols at dusk again found enemy hard at work repairing damage to front line. The Battalion kept up Lewis gun and rifle fire throughout the night.

"16/12/16. Enemy had repaired trenches in the night, but not so effectively as on previous night. Little firing except at 11.30 p.m. and 12 midnight.

"17/12/16. Slow bombardment of enemy position by day. Turkish artillery replied considerably on Central Street and between Emperor's and Queen's Trenches. The Battalion was relieved at 6.5 p.m. by 92nd Punjabis, and marched to No. 1 Camp, Central Area"

By December 18th the 21st Brigade had constructed a model of the Turkish position at Sannaiyat. This was familiarly known as the "hippodrome," and was closely studied by all officers with a view to our forthcoming attack. At 5 p.m. the same day a demonstration was made by the 7th Division against the left of the enemy's position at Sannaiyat. The 28th Brigade, accompanied by the Black Watch and the 20th Punjabis, advanced in full view of the enemy, in artillery formation, along the south edge of the Suwaikiyeh Marsh. The force halted after dark and made considerable noise, clanking entrenching tools, inducing mules to bray, etc., and otherwise attempted to induce the enemy to believe an attack was impending. At the same time battalions in the trenches made similar pretence of great activity. Next morning the troops were back in their original positions, and to their great surprise received the congratulations of their Corps Commander on the success of the operation.

January, 1917.

Early in January, 1917, the 21st Brigade crossed to the right bank of the Tigris. Here it took over various camps and by means of picquets held the whole line of the river trenches from the Narrows to the Sinn Banks. The Battalion moved about from camp to camp all this month, men not engaged in occupying picquets being fully employed in making and repairing roads. In February the 21st Brigade returned to the left bank of the Tigris, and on the 11th were back in the trenches, the Battalion relieving the 57th Rifles.

By this time a new arm had arrived in Mesopotamia—namely, the two-inch trench howitzer. For three days the Battalion was busy digging trenches for them, and on the evening of the 16th moved into the trenches in rear of the Black Watch in readiness to assault next day. At 6.30 a.m. on the 17th orders were received for an attack at noon that day.

Attack on Sannaiyat, February 17th, 1917.

The assault was to be delivered on a two-battalion front, the 1/8th Gurkhas on the right and the 20th Punjabis on the left. The Black Watch were to be in support and the 9th Bhopal Infantry in Brigade reserve. The Battalion had been hard at work carrying up trench mortar shells throughout the 16th and during most of the night 16th-17th, and so were very tired, wet and caked with mud, for during the night heavy rain had fallen and the trenches were knee deep in mud.

Owing to congestion in the trenches, the leading battalions were not in position by noon and the attack was therefore postponed till 2 p.m. The Battalion had only two companies left, the remainder being employed as carrying parties for the two assaulting battalions and for the Brigade Machine Gun Company. At 2 p.m. the two leading battalions advanced after a short bombardment, and reached their objective, the enemy 2nd line, with very little loss. They found many enemy dead from our shelling and most of the survivors sheltering in dug-outs; these they bombed. At 3.9 p.m. forward observation officers reported the enemy massing for a counter-attack, but for some reason our guns did not open fire on this concentration till 3.40 p.m., just as the enemy was leaving his trenches. By the time our guns had fired a few rounds the enemy counter-attack had succeeded. A portion of the 1/8th Gurkhas and the 20th Punjabis were driven back. An immediate counter-attack by our support battalion, the Black Watch, would have saved the situation, but, owing to mud and congested trenches, that unit had not been able to organize and so were unprepared to act. As regards the 9th Bhopal, we had too few men, the remainder, as already stated, being scattered as carrying parties. The enemy counter-attack was not a particularly strong one and ought not to have succeeded. Trench warfare is largely a matter of organization. The whole Brigade was occupying the frontage normally allotted to one battalion, and every communication trench was blocked with carrying parties forming dumps which should have been in position at least twenty-four hours earlier. Confusion consequently and our failure was therefore almost inevitable. Moreover, our artillery was weak and counter-battery work was poor. Of this the Turkish batteries took full advantage. The battery which had been employed on counter-battery tasks for the last month had been relieved on the night 16th-17th, the night before the attack, by one quite new to the sector. Had the attack been postponed for twenty-four hours, there is little doubt it should have succeeded.

On this day some of our Gaur Brahmins formed carrying parties for the Brigade Machine Gun Company, and from all accounts performed their duties most creditably. Two immediate awards were made among them on the strength of the reports submitted by the officers under whom they were serving. Jemadar Jai Lal received the Indian Order of Merit for the fine example he set in handling his platoon, which was acting as carrying party to the Brigade Machine Gun Company. He maintained a sufficient supply of ammunition throughout, and, at a critical time during the counter-attack, he and his platoon engaged the enemy until the machine guns were withdrawn.

No. 237 Sepoy Sheo Chand was with a carrying party and was left behind when our troops were driven back. While making his way back through the enemy trenches he encountered a Turk, whom he promptly captured. He then returned in triumph across "No man's land" with his prisoner, who was almost half as big again as himself.

That night the 21st Brigade was relieved. It marched out at 3.30 a.m., February 18th, and returned to the Central Area, where it spent the next few days preparing for a further attack. This time it was issued with all requisite ammunition, bombs, etc., beforehand. A further attack on the Sannaiyat position was planned for February 22nd. At 6 a.m. on that day the 21st Brigade advanced to a supporting position, where it halted. At 10 a.m. the enemy's position, which had been unsuccessfully

Capture of Sannaiyat, February 22nd, 1917.

attacked on February 17th, was assaulted by the 19th Brigade with complete success. A heavy counter-attack at 12.30 p.m. was caught by our guns, and only three of the enemy reached our lines. At 3.15 p.m. the 28th Brigade attacked and captured the left sector of the enemy's front system. An enemy counter-attack was momentarily successful against the portion of the position held by the 53rd Sikhs, but two companies of the Leicesters advanced and restored the situation. Thus the Sannaiyat position, which had hitherto defied all attacks, had at last fallen into our hands. Throughout the next day the 19th and 28th Brigades continued to make progress, and by evening were occupying the enemy third and fourth lines.

At 9.30 p.m. on the 23rd the 21st Brigade relieved the 19th Brigade. The Black Watch and 9th Bhopals occupied the two front lines and were in position by 3.30 p.m., when patrols were sent forward who reported the enemy's fifth line was abandoned. This was immediately occupied by the Black Watch and the 9th Bhopals.

At dawn further patrols were sent forward from this line, but failed to locate the enemy. At 9 a.m. the 21st Brigade advanced, encountering some slight opposition on its left flank from the retreating enemy. The enemy was not overtaken until Nakhailat, where, after a short and half-hearted resistance, he surrendered. Two Turkish officers and sixty other ranks were captured. At 12.30 p.m. the 21st Brigade reached the Suwada Marsh and halted. Here the Battalion furnished outposts and sent two platoons forward to occupy Saddleback Hill.

Lieutenant B. W. Browning.

On February 22nd at Sannaiyat the casualties of the 19th Brigade were very heavy, and immediate reinforcements of British officers were called for. We had to send Lieutenant B. W. Browning, who was attached to the 92nd Punjabis. He remained with them till he was severely wounded while leading his company in the attack. The 92nd spoke very highly of his gallantry, which mitigated to some extent our sorrow at his loss. Browning was one of the unlucky ones. He was evacuated sick in France on November 17th, 1914, and did not rejoin till March 18th, 1915. In November, 1915, he was accidentally wounded by a bayonet whilst instructing his company in trench warfare in Egypt. On February 15th, 1916, he was back with us for two months, but ill-health again caused his evacuation. He rejoined at the front on February 1st, 1917, and about five weeks later was put *hors de combat* for the rest of the war. He did not pass as medically fit until about May, 1919.

Meanwhile the III Corps, which had been pressing vigorously forward on the right bank of the Tigris, bridged the Dahra Bend on February 23rd, and on the 24th occupied the Shumran Bend. The III Corps and the cavalry thereafter kept the enemy on the run as far as the Diyala River. This proved a formidable obstacle and for a time held up our advance, mainly, however, because we had outrun our supplies. The 7th Division meanwhile pressed on in support, and on the 25th reached Dahra, where it halted until next day. At noon on the 27th it was once more on the move, and by 7.30 p.m. arrived at Shaikh Saad.

By March 7th the 7th Division had reached the famous ruins of Ctesiphon. Here it was that Lieutenant-Colonel Jackson had died with the 6th Division, as previously related. Only a handful of his old comrades were left with us to give him a thought and to wonder whether we were near the spot on which he fell—R.I.P. Next day the Division advanced to Bawi, four miles distant. Here a bridge was in course of construction, and the 7th Division was to be transferred to the right bank. The III Corps (13th and 14th Divisions) and 3rd Division of I Corps were to force the passage of the Diyala, while the 7th Division and Cavalry Brigade were to advance on Baghdad from the west and south-west. The 21st Brigade was ordered to cross the river at 2.30 a.m. on March 9th, but this could not be done, for the enemy had floated a number of rafts downstream, which broke up the bridge. It consequently was 9.30 a.m. before the Brigade, the last Brigade of the Division, actually crossed.

By the afternoon the 19th and 28th Brigades were in action against the enemy covering Baghdad near the ruins of Shawa Khan. The 21st Brigade remained in support all that afternoon and night The 19th and 28th Brigades were having a very arduous time; the enemy had taken up a strong position, and neither brigade could get within eight hundred yards of him. At 6 a.m. on March 10th the 21st Brigade moved up to a position about five hundred yards south-west of the ruins of Shawa Khan, and soon after to a position on the left of the 19th Brigade. Orders for an advance were hourly expected, but none came, and here we remained until dusk, when a general advance was made under cover of darkness. The 21st Brigade followed in support and lay down on the Euphrates—Baghdad railway line for a few hours, during which time a violent dust-storm arose. At 3 a.m. on the 11th the 21st Brigade advanced in column of route towards Baghdad. It moved along the railway with orders to attack the enemy with the bayonet wherever met. No enemy were seen, however, for he, as usual, had retired after dark after attaining his object, which, in this case, was to detain us until his last train from Baghdad had left for Samara.

At dawn the Black Watch and the 9th Bhopals sent out advanced guards on the left and right of the railway line respectively and continued to advance until beyond the northern limit of Kadhimain (the suburb of Baghdad on the right bank). Here the Brigade put out a line of outposts from the river bending back westwards and joined up with the 28th Brigade on our left.

Meanwhile the III Corps had crossed the Diyala on the 10th and advanced on Baghdad along the left bank.

CHAPTER XVIII.

OPERATIONS SUBSEQUENT TO THE FALL OF BAGHDAD.

(See Map facing page 120.)

ON March 12th the intention was to send a force to Felujah on the Euphrates. The 9th Bhopals had actually moved to the starting point when the march was cancelled, as available transport did not allow of the carriage of water and rations for the column. Apparently our information about the route was refuted by the American Consul, and it was therefore decided that a cavalry reconnaissance was necessary before sending a column. The enemy retiring up the Euphrates from Samawa did not pass Felujah for some days after we reached Baghdad. Had the original plan been possible of achievement he might not have escaped at all. Shortage of transport was a severe handicap for the remainder of this season's campaign. When one corps operated the other was rendered practically immobile, as all its transport had to be borrowed. Hitherto operations had been confined to the immediate vicinity of the Tigris, and river transport had supplied the force to a large extent. Conditions were now changed; the enemy was widely scattered, and our troops operating against him had to depend almost entirely on land transport. It was necessary therefore to limit the scope of operations and to concentrate on the particular front which was the most important at the moment. The Samara railway was the immediate danger spot, since the enemy had successfully evacuated all rolling stock and was in a position to concentrate against Baghdad. General Maude therefore decided to advance along the railway line in order to remove, as far as possible, this threat.

We can now turn to the part played by the Battalion in the subsequent operations. At 9.30 p.m. on March 13th the 7th Division resumed its advance, moving in the following order:—28th Brigade, 21st Brigade, Divisional Headquarters, 19th Brigade.

Action at Mushahida. *(See Map facing p. 120.)*

Northwards of Baghdad the ground was of a different character. For fourteen months the Battalion had lived on a dead flat plain composed of sand and clay, without even a tree to relieve the monotony. On one occassion, while digging at Sannaiyat, to our great surprise a pebble was found—it is doubtful whether the discovery of a gold nugget would have caused more comment. Now, we were on undulating ground, and further north came to rock and along the river bank actual bluffs up to 40 feet high.

After a halt of two hours at dawn the advance was resumed, the 21st Brigade moving in line of companies in fours. With frequent halts this formation continued until about noon when the Brigade crossed the Baghdad—Samara railway. After crossing the railway, units of the 21st Brigade deployed into artillery formation, the right of the Black Watch rested on the railway line, the 1/8th Gurkhas being on their left and the 9th Bhopals in echelon on the left of the 1/8th Gurkhas in brigade reserve.

The divisional plan for the attack on Mushahida Station was to attack with two brigades astride the railway, which was to form the dividing line ; the 28th Brigade was on the right, the 21st Brigade on the left, and the 19th Brigade in echelon on the left of the 21st Brigade, in divisional reserve. Cavalry were operating somewhere on our left flank, but we saw no sign of them.

The enemy's position extended from the river on his left to some high ground (afterwards named Bhopal Hill) about 1,000 yards west of the railway. Our advance was across a bare plain, but a slight ridge some 1,200 yards distant from and parallel to the enemy's position offered some slight cover. A few mounds here and there also afforded some shelter for our guns. Conditions this day were unfavourable for the 7th Division. The troops had been on the move almost continuously for eighteen hours, carrying greatcoats and packs, and water was scarce. As a result progress was slow and a comparatively small force of the enemy was able to inflict about 700 casualties on the Division and hold it up until his train had departed from Mushahida Station and darkness covered his retreat.

As previously stated, the Battalion was in brigade reserve. When our leading companies (" B " and " C ") reached the ridge already mentioned, they realized that by continuing in the same direction they could outflank the enemy. This information they at once passed back, and sanction was obtained from Brigade Headquarters to send them on this mission.

"B" and "C" Companies advanced at 4 p.m., and soon came under somewhat heavy, long-range rifle fire. Lieutenant D. F. Hubert, who was commanding "C" Company, was hit, shortly afterwards dying. These two companies continued to make ground, however, and before dark reported that they were in position on the enemy's flank facing east. Brigade Headquarters was informed, and the Battalion's reserve companies, supported by an intense artillery bombardment from 6.25 to 6.30 p.m., were ordered to attack the hill on which the enemy's right flank rested. Speaking on the telephone, just before this attack started, General Norie was doubtful of being able to arrange the bombardment, as his telephone line to the artillery had just been taken up in readiness for an advance. He said, however, he would do his best to arrange it. "A" and "D" Companies advanced against the hill. Light was failing fast, and they reached the foot of the hill with very few casualties. By 6.30 p.m. the bombardment had not taken place, hence it was assumed that the Brigade Commander had not been able to arrange it. It was therefore decided to rush the hill at once. This was done, and on arrival on the top, the enemy was found to have fled, leaving behind a few wounded. It was now quite dark, and companies had just begun to reorganize when our own artillery commenced their five-minute bombardment. The men took cover in the enemy trenches, but before our guns had ceased fire, had suffered some twenty casualties. The Battalion were ordered to remain on the hill for the night.

Capture of Bhopal Hill.

The Battalion's total casualties in this action were:—1 British officer and 12 other ranks killed, and 60 other ranks wounded. Lieutenant D. F. Hubert was deeply mourned by all ranks. He was an exceptionally promising young officer who would have gone far in the service had he lived. Besides being capable, he possessed the gift of endearing himself to all with whom he came in contact. The stretcher party who brought his body in to Battalion Headquarters were weeping bitterly. Amongst the wounded were Subedars Rahmat Ali Khan and Mohar Singh. The former joined the Battalion in France as a havildar with the reinforcements of the 5th Infantry. He was a very good Indian officer and a great loss to the company.

Casualties.

For the next two days the Brigade was occupied in clearing the battlefield. We had learnt that the Arab habitually disinterred corpses for the sake of their clothing, and we therefore levelled every grave thoroughly and then marched a body of men over it to render it indistinguishable from its surroundings. This work completed, the Brigade moved to the river near Beit Nawab, and thereafter patrolled the river bends as the flood season was at hand.

Baghdad.

On March 25th the Brigade returned to Baghdad to its old quarters on the right bank. Here it was rejoined by the 20th Punjabis, and all four units took their regular turn of duty on the outpost line. During the next few days all ranks took every occasion that offered of visiting the city. The town is very picturesque and full of interest, while the bazaars afforded the whole force ample opportunities of spending good money to buy trash. The Baghdad shopkeeper was not slow to open his doors when order was restored and in those early days reaped a rich harvest by which he doubtless recouped himself after the trying times he had lately endured. For many months past we had been living on bare army rations; here we enjoyed an ample supply of fresh vegetables and oranges, as luscious as could be found.

Alas! the joys of town life were not long our portion, for the next phase of the campaign was soon to begin. The objective was the railhead at Samara, and advance was to be along both banks of the River Tigris. On the right bank a force, consisting of the 7th Division and additional artillery, and, on the left bank a force under General Marshall. On April 4th, at 7 p.m., the Battalion received orders to march, one company ("C") to Hassaiwa, one company ("D") and Headquarters to Babi, about twenty-one miles distant, and two companies ("A" and "B") to Fort Kermea, about thirty-three miles distant.

By April 9th the 28th Brigade had captured Balad Station and, on this day, Harba, the adjoining station. Here a lucky haul of over 200 railway wagons was made; these, drawn by animals were a welcome addition to the existing transport during the subsequent advance.

On the right bank of the river the enemy had retired to Istabulat, and was preparing a position covering the station. This he was able to do at his leisure, as we were unable to advance until the situation on the left bank had been cleared up.

MAP NO 6

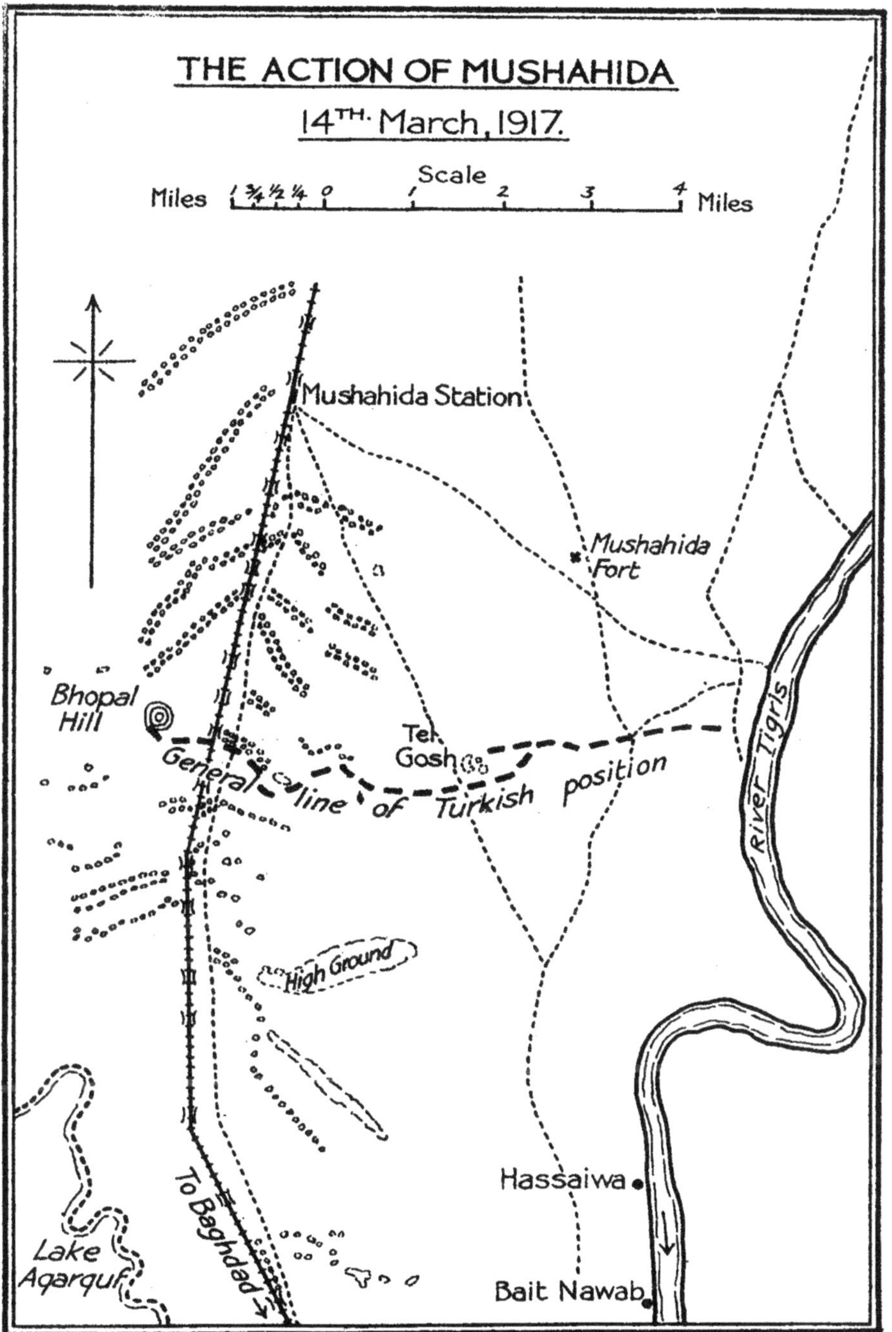

BY PERMISSION OF THE CONTROLLER OF H.M. STATIONERY OFFICE

On the evening of the 11th the Battalion Headquarters, with "A" and "B" Companies, moved at 5.30 p.m. to join the Brigade at Balad, eighteen miles distant, "C" and "D" Companies remaining another two days at Fort Kermea, before rejoining. By the evening of April 14th the 21st Brigade was concentrated, and next day marched to Harba, four miles to the north.

The Battle of Istabulat. (*See Map facing p.* 124.)

On April 16th the Turkish outpost position covering Istabulat was driven in and the 21st Brigade occupied a line of sandhills at Mustabba. The next day this ridge was occupied by the 9th Bhopals as an outpost position covering the Brigade; the 9th Bhopals remaining on outpost until the night of April 20th-21st. By this time the situation on the left bank of the Tigris had been cleared up enabling the 7th Division to advance northwards. The 7th Division Commander decided to attack the Turkish Istabulat position without delay. The 19th Brigade was to attack to the west of the Dujail Canal, the 21st to the east, while the 28th Brigade was to remain in reserve.

The front that the 21st Brigade had to advance over consisted of a rough triangle of high ground, whose base roughly equalled the frontage of two battalions—the Black Watch and the 1/8th Gurkhas. The left was bounded by the Dujail canal, which at this point was sunken some feet below the level of the plateau. The right of the triangle was bounded by a steep bank which leads on to the low ground, bordering the river, some eight feet below the level of the plateau. The 9th Bhopals were to advance along this low ground under cover of the bank. The Turks occupied the apex of the triangle. By 3 a.m. on April 21st the Battalion was withdrawn from outpost duty, and, at 5.30 a.m., the 21st Brigade advanced to the attack. At 6.30 a.m. the Black Watch and 1/8th Gurkhas were held up on the line *A—B* by heavy rifle and machine-gun fire from the Turkish position some 500 yards to their front (line *GH*). The 9th Bhopals continued to advance under cover of the bank on their left, and by 7 a.m. had reached point *D*, thereby cutting off the retreat of the Turks in redoubt *H*. The Turks thereupon surrendered to the Gurkhas who captured some 200 prisoners.

At 7.30 a.m. the Black Watch and 1/8th Gurkhas were again held up, this time on the line *G—H*, by fire from redoubt *J* and from Turkish trenches about the point *O*. The supporting artillery on the capture of redoubt *H* had moved forward, and was therefore unable to support a further attack for some time. The 9th Bhopals continued to advance under cover of the high ground, and when level with redoubt *J* came under ineffective fire from trenches at point *Y*. On reaching point *E*, "A" and "B" Companies came under very heavy machine-gun fire from point *P*. Almost immediately three out of the four British officers present were wounded, and "A" and "B" Companies lost over seventy-five per cent. of their strength. Major Irvine, Commanding the Battalion, Captain Banks, Adjutant, and Captain Roberts, commanding "B" Company, were thus put out of action. The remaining British officer, Captain Rodwell, was in rear commanding "D" Company. Without British officers there was great confusion, and the forward companies were beginning to waver when Subedar-Major Govind Singh collected the remnants of "A" and "B" Companies and extended them to the right, where the low scrub afforded a certain amount of protection. Meanwhile, "C" and "D" Companies, who still were under cover, extended behind "A" and "B" Companies and endeavoured to support the leading companies. Almost immediately the enemy threatened to counter-attack from point *T*. Realizing that he would have a better chance to meet this from the high ground, Subedar-Major Govind Singh rushed "A" and "B" Companies to their left on to the high ground where they occupied some vacant trenches at *R*

Heavy Casualties.

A message was now received from the 1/8th Gurkhas to the effect that the Turks were advancing from the direction of redoubt *J*, and that there was a gap of nearly 1,000 yards between them and the 9th Bhopals. The Turkish attack did not, however, materialize, but the position of the 1/9th Bhopals was considered too precarious to be maintained. "A" and "B" Companies, besides losing seventy-five per cent. of their effectives, had only one serviceable Lewis gun between them. It was accordingly decided to withdraw the Battalion in order to regain touch with the 1/8th Gurkhas preparatory to the next co-ordinated attack by the Brigade. "C" Company was ordered to man the crestline of the high ground and to cover the withdrawal of the rest of the Battalion. This withdrawal was accomplished at the cost of very few casualties, and by 9.45 a.m., the Battalion, less "C" Company, was reorganizing in the deep nullah west of the redoubt *H*. A platoon of "C" Company remained near point *D*, and at 10 a.m. were joined by the remainder of this company. The remainder of the Battalion was ordered to be prepared to advance at 11 a.m. under cover of an artillery barrage and come up on the right of the 1/8th Gurkhas. This was duly accomplished, and the remainder of the Battalion was then connected up with "C" Company.

About noon the enemy was reported to be concentrating on the river bank east of point *Y*, and a flank attack from the north appeared likely. To meet this our two left companies were withdrawn and sent to occupy positions about point *B*. The 20th Punjabis were then called upon to fill the gap between the 1/8th Gurkhas and our companies at and near point *D*. At nightfall two companies of the 53rd Sikhs (28th Brigade) relieved the two left companies of the 9th Bhopals at point *B*, and these two companies then rejoined the remainder of the Battalion at point *D*. At 8 p.m. the Battalion sent out a strong patrol to work along the Tigris as far as the Dujail. This patrol returned at 2 a.m. having accomplished its mission and reported that the whole area was clear of the enemy. A second patrol, sent out immediately, confirmed this report.

At 4 a.m. on the 22nd the Battalion had orders to support a dawn attack by the 53rd Sikhs on the front, *P—J*. As previously reported by our patrols, the enemy had withdrawn and the Dujail was crossed unopposed.

The various moves of the companies early in this engagement are difficult to piece together, for over two hours there was only one British officer present, and the Battalion was badly disorganized through casualties. Platoon commanders, many of whom were non-commissioned officers, acted largely on their own initiative, and were unable to give detailed descriptions of their moves. Only after reorganization by Lieutenant Rodwell, at about 9.30 a.m. on the 21st, does a connected narrative emerge. By that time the Brigade had expended its energy, and there was practically no forward movement after the advance under cover of a barrage at 11 a.m.

Casualties this day were very heavy, the Battalion lost over fifty per cent. of its effectives, somewhere about 260 were killed and wounded. Captain Banks was being carried back on a stretcher when a second shot killed him. A gallant, very capable officer, cheery under the most trying conditions and a general favourite; his loss was deeply felt by all. Major Irvine's condition was favourably reported on from Baghdad; later he was evacuated to Amara, where his wound unfortunately became septic, and he eventually died. The news was a bitter blow to the dwindling band of survivors of those distant, peaceful days before the war. Captain Roberts rejoined the Battalion some months later and remained with it until demobilized in 1919.

Casualties.

Meanwhile, the remainder of the 7th Division advanced along the Dujail and came up with the enemy in a position covering Istabulat Police Station. After several hours' hard fighting he was dislodged, and the 21st Brigade, which was in divisional reserve, reached the police station by 7 p.m. At 6.30 a.m. on the 23rd the advance was resumed. The 21st Brigade led, and the Black Watch and 9th Bhopals formed the advance guard. The gilded dome of the mosque at Samara glittered in the morning sunlight and made an excellent landmark on which to march. But none was needed, for the enemy had decamped in a hurry, and a trail of papers, empty ammunition boxes and rubbish of every description was visible as far as the eye could reach. Amongst all this rubbish a piece of paper was picked up which gave us definite information. This was a memo from Turkish Headquarters to one of the regimental commanders, informing him of the next rendezvous and instructing him not to be late on this occasion. The rendezvous in question was a point many miles north of Samara.

Samara.

We arrived at Samara Railway Station at noon, and halted. The 19th Brigade passed through us and occupied an outpost position on the high ground some two miles north of Samara The remainder of the Division encamped on the bank of the river. The town of Samara is situated on the left bank of the River Tigris, and on April 25th a detachment of 100 rifles each from the Black Watch and the 9th Bhopals was ferried across for its protection. The Battalion's total casualties at Istabulat were more than replaced by two drafts which joined on April 25th and 28th respectively. No further advance was contemplated

MAP No.7

Istabulat
Railway
Station
To Istabulat 5 Miles
P
T
Y
R. Tigris
E
R
J
Dujail Canal
M
G
O
D
A
H
Low lying
ground
covered in scrub
liable to
inundation.
B
High earth bank.
R. Tigris
Mushabba
Sketch to illustrate
the action of ISTABULAT
21ST. April 1917
TURKISH TRENCHES
Scale
Yards 1500 1000 500 0 1 2 Miles

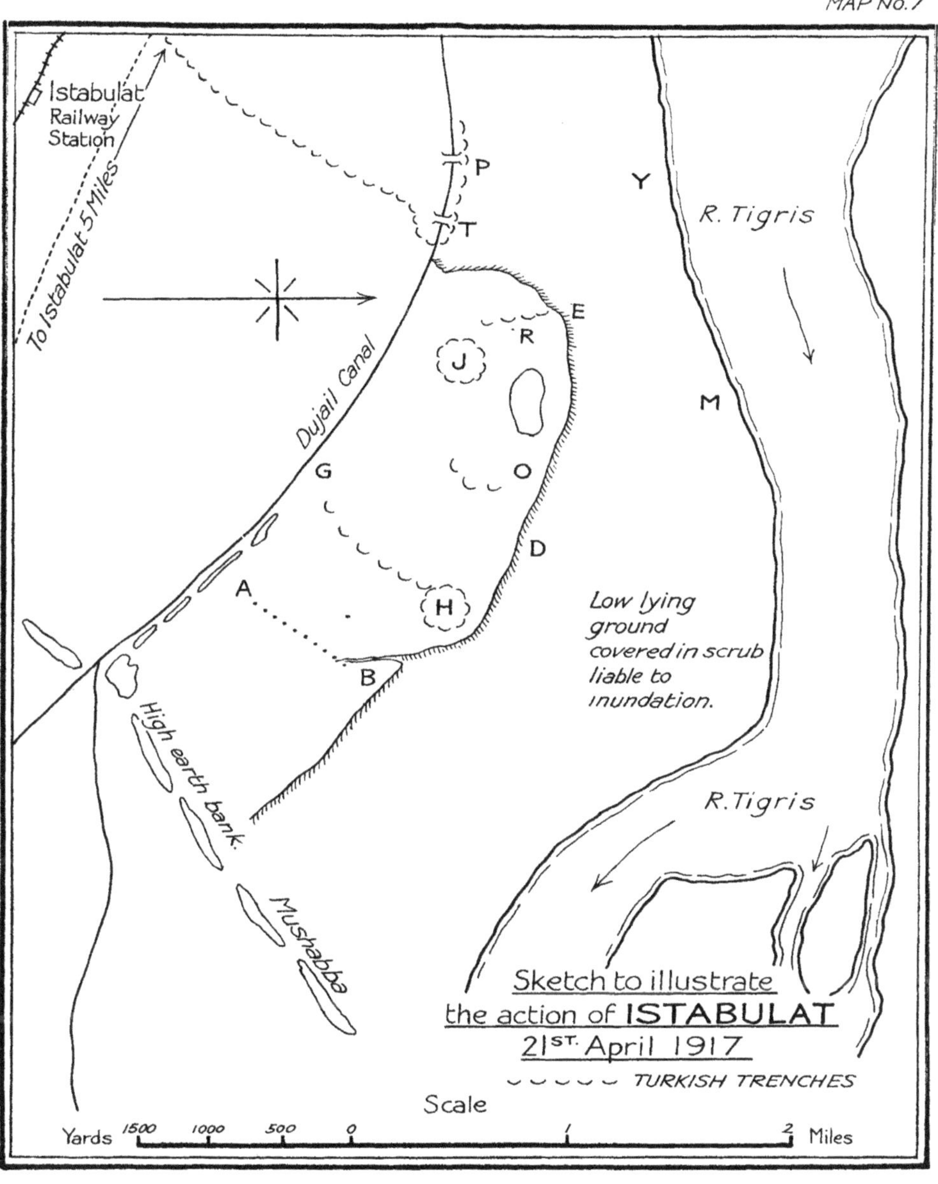

for the present in this section ; the 7th Division therefore occupied a defensive position on both sides of the river about four miles north of Samara Railway Station. A few days later the Battalion was relieved by the Guides Infantry and was withdrawn for duty on the lines of communication.

CHAPTER XIX.

MAY, 1917, TO MARCH, 1919.

THE Battalion left Samara on May 4th. On leaving, the Divisional and Brigade Commanders were present to say good-bye, and expressed their appreciation of the good work done by the Battalion whilst under their command and the hope that they would soon see it back under them again. This hope was never fulfilled; for the Battalion continued on the lines of communication until December, 1918. During this period the war diary is interesting only for the occasional flashes of humour with which different Adjutants varied the monotony of the statement that there was nothing to report.

Duties on the Lines of Communication.

From Samara to Balad the Battalion marched along the railway line, kits being carried in trucks drawn by the first line mules. From Balad the Battalion crossed to Fort Kermea, where it took steamer to Baghdad and then to Shaikh Saad, where it eventually halted and undertook guards and duties. Two months later the Battalion moved up to Kut, where Battalion Headquarters remained until October, 1918. Its duties here were purely defensive. Kut, being the starting point for a railway which followed the left bank of the Tigris to Baghdad, therefore contained a large camp. Protection was afforded by barbed wire defences joining up numerous small posts at intervals of a quarter of a mile. The total perimeter was over four miles long, and all posts were occupied by night. By day only the posts at the various exits were occupied.

Towards the end of November, 1917, a party of 6 Indian officers and 17 non-commissioned officers were sent to Fyzabad to join the 3/9th Bhopal Infantry which was being raised. Early in March, 1918, a call was made for yet more of our dwindling band of old soldiers. Two Indian officers and 81 non-commissioned officers and men were sent to Fyzabad as a nucleus for the newly-raised 4/9th Bhopal Infantry.

In June, 1918, a complete company of Rajputs were sent to India to join the 2/150th Infantry. With it went Captain Newman, much to the regret of all whom he left behind;

he had been with the Battalion over two years and was a confirmed optimist at all times.

After the Rajput company had left, the Battalion was reorganized on an experimental basis of class platoons instead of class companies. The organization was as follows :—

" A " Company :—

No. 1 Platoon ... ... Sikhs.
No. 2 Platoon ... ... Gaur Brahmins.
No. 3 Platoon ... ... Muhammadans
No. 4 Platoon ... ... Gaur Brahmins.

" B " Company :—

No. 5 Platoon ... ... Gaur Brahmins.
No. 6 Platoon ... ... Rajputs.
No. 7 Platoon ... ... Gaur Brahmins.
No. 8 Platoon ... ... Brahmins.

" C " Company :—

No. 9 Platoon ... ... Gaur Brahmins.
No. 10 Platoon ... ... Brahmins.
No. 11 Platoon ... ... Muhammadans.
No. 12 Platoon ... ... Rajputs.

" D " Company :—

No. 13 Platoon ... ... Gaur Brahmins.
No. 14 Platoon ... ... Gaur Brahmins.
No. 15 Platoon ... ... Muhammadans.
No. 16 Platoon ... ... Sikhs.

In October, 1918, the Battalion received orders to relieve the 83rd Infantry at Basra, and embarked on the P.S. 93 on the 10th. This move came just in time to stamp out influenza, which had begun to assume serious proportions in the Battalion, and a week after reaching Basra we were absolutely free. A second outbreak in November was similarly suppressed, and an idea consequently took root among us that a change of air was the best means of defeating this scourge.

Battalion joins 42nd Brigade at Ramadie.

Early in November news was received that the 3/9th Bhopal Infantry were on their way from India to relieve the Battalion and that we would then join the III Corps. The Battalion moved upstream in two steamers and reached Baghdad on the 30th. From there it marched to Ramadie on the Euphrates, arriving on December 7th and being then posted to the 42nd Brigade, 15th Division, in place of 2/5th Gurkhas.

Here, when not engaged in fatigue or duties, the men were employed in making bricks. If results had been commensurate with the energy expended, it might have been said that Ramadie possessed the best set of barracks in Mesopotamia. But, as drying shelters were not available, half a week's work was often washed away by one day's rain. On this profitable employment we were engaged until we received the joyful tidings of an early return to India.

On March 1st the Battalion left Ramadie by road, and on March 14th was in Basra, after a sojourn of over three years in Mesopotamia. Except in name, it was practically a new Battalion, for of those who had disembarked at Basra on December 21st, 1915, only 2 British officers, 3 Indian officers and 60 other ranks survived. May those whom were left behind rest in peace in the assurance that their sacrifice was not in vain and that the example they set inspired their successors to win fresh laurels for the 9th Bhopals.

Return to India.

En route from Bombay to Fyzabad, the Battalion halted for one day at Bhopal. Here the train was met by Colonel Nawab Muhammad Nasurullah Khan and officials of Bhopal State. At the station were also many pensioners who had served in the Battalion in the days when it was a local unit and recruited small numbers in the state. On detraining, the men were marched to a camp where they were sumptuously fed, later they were taken round the city. British officers were taken to the Rest House and Indian officers to the Shargat Mahal. During the afternoon all officers were presented to Her Highness the Begum. In the evening British officers were entertained at a State banquet.

Next morning at 9 a.m. the Battalion left for Fyzabad. It was good to be home again after an absence of over four and a half years, and better still to know that throughout those strenuous years all ranks had worthily upheld the traditions of the 9th Bhopal Infantry and of the Indian Army.

Postscript by Colonel H. H. Smith, D.S.O.

" There is one point that I should like to bring to notice, that is the paucity of our honours. I know many Commanding Officers submitted names and obtained decoration for their men for work which was undeserving to say the least.

" I, myself (as I now think) in Mesopotamia rather went on the other tack. I know there were many instances of good work which went unrecorded. It was not through want of appreciation on my part, but because I felt that we were only doing our duty as we were expected to. There are two ways of looking at the matter, and I should like to make a record of this in the Regimental History."

MAP NO. 8.

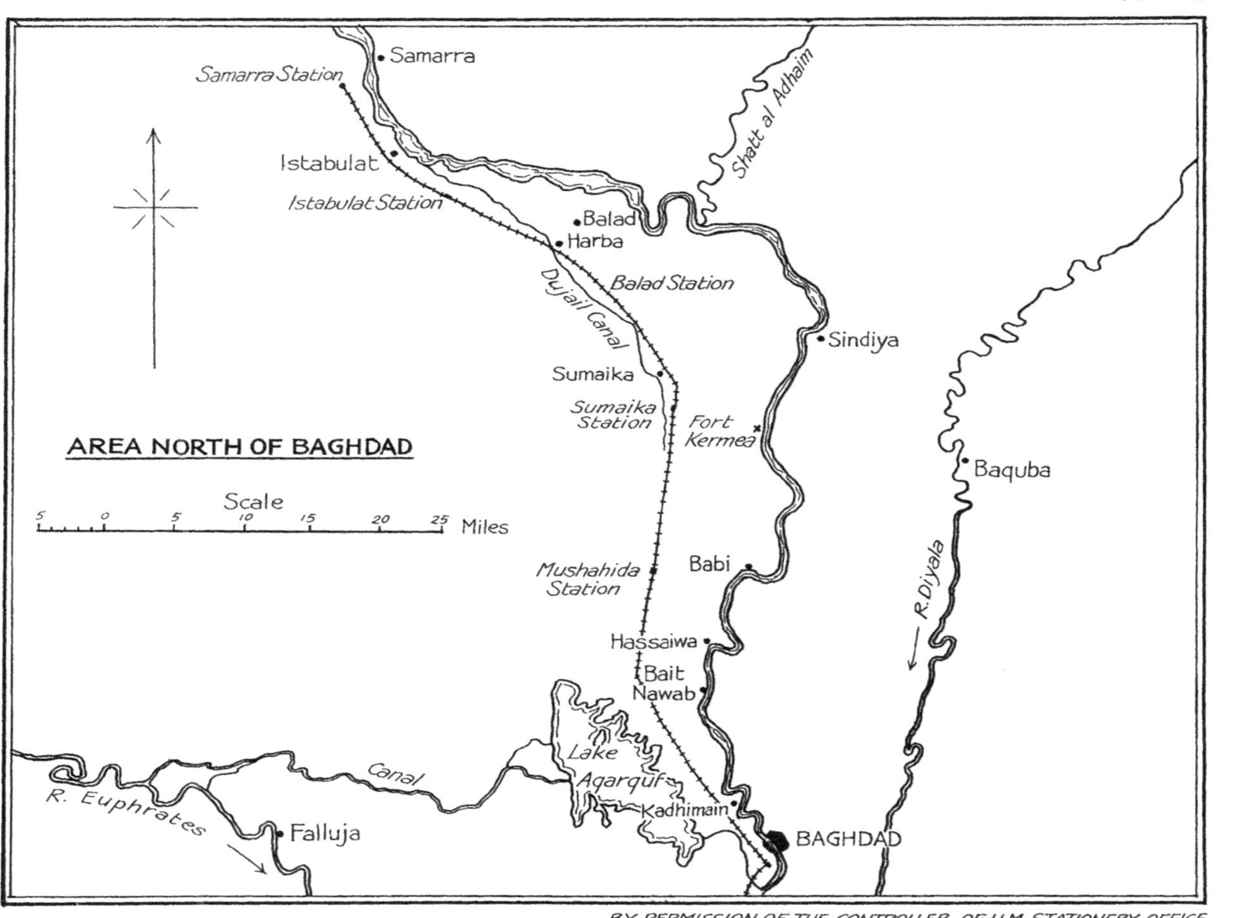

BY PERMISSION OF THE CONTROLLER OF H.M. STATIONERY OFFICE

Part V.

1919 to 1930.

CHAPTER XX

1919 TO 1930.

ON March 20th, 1919, the Battalion returned from field service in Mesopotamia to Fyzabad in the Central Provinces some one thousand men strong. Of the original Battalion who left Fyzabad in August, 1914, no British officer and only some fifteen Sikhs and Muhammadans returned with it.

Throughout the war the Depot of the Battalion had remained at Fyzabad. The Depot, from its original establishment of 200, had grown enormously ; in 1917 it numbered 2,000, and at this time (1919) it numbered about 1,200. Besides helping to keep the Battalion supplied with reinforcements in the field, the Depot had the task of providing the nucleus of the 2nd Bn. 9th Delhi Regiment and the 3rd and 4th Battalions of the 9th Bhopal Infantry. At one time during the war there were some 12,000 men on its books. To increase the training staff of the Depot pensioned Indian officers and non-commissioned officers had been employed. These, though no longer fit for service in the field, proved invaluable for training recruits. Among the Indian officers who rejoined was ex-Subedar-Major Sheikh Ali Mohammed, whose ardour had in no way been quenched during his retirement on pension.

Battalion recalled from Furlough.

Those officers who returned from Mesopotamia and who were looking forward to a quiet life in cantonments were soon to be disillusioned. The first month was spent in sending Indian officers and non-commissioned officers on pension and discharging recruits, while all soldiers who had been on service were sent on their well-earned furlough. Hardly had these men proceeded on furlough, when they had to be recalled owing to the outbreak of war with Afghanistan. By the beginning of May the Battalion was again mobilized and was immediately employed on railway security duties.

" A " and " D " Companies were sent to Delhi to guard the Great Indian Peninsular Railway from Delhi to Agra. " B " and " C " Companies were sent to Allahabad and

Moghul Serai on similar duties. Battalion headquarters moved to Delhi, while the Depot, which had not yet been demobilized, remained at Fyzabad.

The Battalion spent the whole of the hot weather of 1919 split up in detachments and during this time frequent inspections provided the only relief from monotony.

In September the Battalion was once more concentrated in Fyzabad and the men sent off again on furlough. Five months later it was once more together, and in February, 1920, proceeded to join the 46th Brigade, Kohat-Kurram Field Force, at Kohat. It was a matter of great regret to all that by some few weeks only the Battalion missed the grant of the Afghan War Medal, 1919-1920. At Kohat duties and picquets were very heavy; night alarms were of frequent occurrence, and our stay there was under field service conditions.

Service in Kohat.

In June of this year (1920) the Battalion saw the departure of Subedar-Major Govind Singh Bahadur. Govind Singh was one of the few who had been lucky in the Great War. He remained with "A" Company almost continuously throughout the four and a half years of the war. He was twice wounded, but his absences from the field were of very short duration. During the early days of 1916 in Mesopotamia, when the Battalion was living in a sea of icy-cold mud, all British officers who were there will remember his cheery optimism and the frequent mugs of tea that he and his company used to produce at all hours of the night. The writer has reason to remember one morning at dawn, after a particularly wet night in the open in April, 1916, when Govind Singh produced his water bottle entirely full of rum. Captain Govind Singh (his present rank) still takes a keen interest in the Battalion, and visits his old Battalion and the Training Battalion once or twice a year.

Captain Govind Singh.

In August, 1920, the Battalion was sent to Hangu in the Kohat area, with detachments at Fort Lockhart, Fort Gulistan and Sangar Post. At this time the Battalion was organized on the class platoon system, and consisted of four platoons of Sikhs, four platoons of Gaur Brahmins, two platoons of Eastern Brahmins, two platoons of Rajput Muhammadans, two platoons of Hindustani Muhammadans and two platoons of Rajputs.

Service in Hangu.

Reorganization. In the following March the whole of the Indian Army was reorganized and considerably reduced. Our new composition now consisted of :—

"A" Company	... ...	Sikhs.
"B" Company	... ...	Punjabi Muhammadans.
"C" Company	... ...	Punjabi Muhammadans.
"D" Company	... ...	Rajput Dogras.

Punjabi Muhammadans were to be recruited from Jhelum, Rawal Pindi, Campbellpur, Shahpur, Poonch and the Murree Hills; actually the Battalion took men from only the first three districts. The Dogras were to be enlisted from Kangra, Hoshiarpore, Sialkote districts and from Jammu State. The majority of Dogras being enlisted from the first two districts.

The 1/9th (now once again the 9th) Bhopal Infantry was included in the 16th Group, Indian Infantry, the other battalions being the 30th, the 31st, the 33rd Punjabis and the 40th Pathans. The last battalion was shortly after changed to another group and the 46th Punjabis became our Training Battalion. The new composition meant that of the old Battalion only the Sikhs were retained. The reorganization of the Battalion was completed in September, 1921. This had been done by transferring full formations to and from other battalions whose composition had likewise altered. A summary of these transfers is as follows :—

(1) *Punjabi Muhammadans.*—One complete company was received from the 1/25th Punjabis. Two platoons were received from the 1/153rd Infantry. One platoon was received from the 1/19th Punjabis. One platoon was received from the 3/124th Baluchis. A total of two companies.

(2) *Dogras.*—One and a half platoons were received from the 31st Punjabis. One and a half platoons were received from the 52nd Sikhs. One platoon was received from the 1/25th Punjabis. A total of one company.

(3) About two platoons of original Muhammadans were transferred to the 1/10th Jats and the 112th Infantry. All the Gaur Brahmins, Rajputs, Eastern Brahmins and the Hindustani Muhammadans were demobilized.

Service in Ambala.

In September, 1921, a Headquarter Wing was formed in each battalion of the Indian Army. This system, now (in 1930), seems so familiar and sensible that one wonders why no one thought of it before. In the same month the Battalion received orders to proceed to the Persian Gulf in the following March. With the exception of a small depot, all the men were sent off on three and a half months' furlough from Hangu. On October 15th this depot, with all the baggage of the Battalion, entrained with great difficulty for Ambala. The difficulty referred to was caused by a particularly virulent type of fever associated with Hangu. Before we left some eighty per cent. of the men were suffering from this fever, and only the small capacity of the hospital prevented their being admitted there. Its stay in Ambala was limited to four months. The only point worthy of notice during this time was the presence in the Battalion of fifteen British officers, compared to the strength of the depot of thirty men. Most of these officers were awaiting demobilization, and had been sent from the 2/9th Delhi Regiment and the 3rd and 4th Battalions 9th Bhopal Infantry who had been demobilized.

Service in the Persian Gulf.

The Battalion arrived in the Persian Gulf on February 25th, 1922, and was distributed along the coast in detachments. "B" Company was sent to Charbar, Muscat, Jask and Bahrein. "C" Company was sent to Bandar Abbas, Henjam and Kishm. Battalion Headquarters and the remaining two companies went to Bushire with small posts in the city and at Sabzadad.

Abolition of the Brass Band.

In September, 1922, it was decided to do away with the brass band. It was found that the expenses incurred in maintaining it during and after the war had increased enormously, and that good musicians could only be obtained by paying them very highly. Furthermore, the absence of all playing-out engagements during the war and at the frontier and overseas stations we had been stationed at in the past three years, and were likely to be sent to in the future, meant that the cost of maintaining it devolved entirely on the British officers. With the band we said farewell to our Bandmaster, Lieutenant A. C. Webb. Mr. Webb joined us in 1906 after serving twenty-one years in the Oxford and

Buckinghamshire Light Infantry, and his work during the Great War is worthy of note. In September, 1914, the original band went with the Battalion to France as stretcher-bearers; there they quickly became casualties. Mr. Webb, who remained in the Depot, trained a new band out of the band boys and unfit musicians. This band was ready by the end of 1915, and in October, 1916, was sent, as a band, to the 7th Divisional Headquarters in Mesopotamia. Mr. Webb himself accompanied them, and while in Mesopotamia obtained a commission in the Labour Corps. On the return of the Battalion from Mesopotamia most of the band took their discharge. So that the band that was disbanded in 1922 contained very few of the old musicians. A drum and pipe band was started to replace the brass band.

Mess Dress.

Up to this time the Mess dress for the Battalion was the old braided drab dress. In December, 1922, in order to conform with the other battalions of the 16th Infantry Group, a new Mess dress was decided on which was as under :—

Mess Jacket.—Scarlet cloth, roll collar, pointed cuffs, small buttons down the front and on the sleeves and shoulder-straps. White facings on jacket and cuffs, and jacket edged with white piping.

Mess Vest.—White, with four small buttons.

Overalls.—Blue cloth with scarlet welt one quarter of an inch wide.

Boots.—Wellington, with box spurs for mounted officers.

The old badges of the 9th Bhopal Infantry, the fish, continued to be worn for a few years.

The 4th Battalion 16th Punjab Regiment.

In December of this year (1922) the name of the Battalion was once more changed. We now became the 4th Battalion of the 16th Punjab Regiment. The other battalions of the group likewise changed their name. The 30th Punjabis became the 1st Battalion; the 31st Punjabis became the 2nd Battalion; the 33rd Punjabis became the 3rd Battalion, and the 46th Punjabis became the 10th or Training Battalion. In losing the title of Bhopal, a tradition of over one hundred years was broken. With the loss of this title our connection with the Bhopal State gradually disappeared. Incidentally it may be mentioned that we had been more generally known throughout the Army as " The Bo-peeps."

Service in Jubbulpore.

In April, 1923, the Battalion went to Jubbulpore, and it was not until October, when the men returned from furlough, that the Battalion was all together for the first time since their reorganization. Its stay in Jubbulpore lasted only two years. During this short time " A " Company (Sikhs) won the Brigade Hockey Tournament twice, and the Tug-of-War Cup ; the Battalion won the Central Provinces District Efficiency Competition and Bayonet Fencing, while No. 9 Platoon, under Jemadar Ghulam Mohammed, won the District Efficiency Cup. The Battalion went on annual manœuvres at Saugor in 1924 and to Nimkhera Camp in 1925. In Jubbulpore opportunities for shikar were good. The Battalion had a forest block some twelve miles south of cantonments known as the " Dhobi Block." During the time it was in Jubbulpore ten tigers, five panthers and two bison were shot.

In February, 1924, Colonel H. H. Smith, D.S.O., retired, and command of the Battalion devolved on Major R. W. Gaskell. Colonel Smith commanded the Battalion for a period of nearly ten years. He virtually commanded the Battalion in Mesopotamia from April, 1916, to the end of its stay there.

Service in Waziristan.

Next month the Battalion left for Razani in Waziristan. It trained to Bannu via the ferry at Mari-Indus and marched to Razani, where it joined the 9th Infantry Brigade. Life at Razani was strenuous and training was good. The Battalion was in permanent picquets one month and out on road protection duties the next month.

In December, 1925, the Battalion was transferred to Razmak. where it remained until the end of its tour in Waziristan. During this time it twice went out on Brigade movable column, and during August and September was out on a bridging column at Tauda China. Throughout its tour the Battalion did not lose a man, rifle or round of ammunition.

In the year 1924-1925 the Battalion won the Francis Memorial Cup for the best revolver shooting team among all units in the Indian Army. The Battalion won the cup again the following year and, for the third year in succession, in 1926-1927. Unfortunately the cup cannot be won outright, a replica of it was, however, presented to the Mess.

Service in Ahmedabad.

In November, 1926, the Battalion proceeded to Ahmedabad, in the Bombay District, where it remained for four years. "C" and "D" Companies marched the last four hundred miles of the journey, detraining at Kotah and marching via Chitorgarh and Udaipur.

Lieutenant-Colonel G. D. Martin, M.C.

In February, 1929, Lieutenant-Colonel R. W. Gaskell retired and the command of the Battalion devolved on Lieutenant-Colonel G. D. Martin, M.C. A few weeks after taking over, the latter died from internal hæmorrhage. The loss of Colonel Martin came as a great shock to the Battalion and was greatly felt by all. During the twenty five years he served with the Battalion, he continually endeavoured to improve the lot of the sepoy, and he will be always remembered for the work he did in this connection. He was the last survivor of the Sehore days. He was Adjutant of the Battalion during the first three years of the war, and was lucky enough not to be wounded severely, never leaving the theatre of operations for four and a half years. All ranks insisted on subscribing towards the cost of his tombstone which was erected in Ahmedabad.

Lieutenant-Colonel C. N. Steel arrived from the 1st Battalion 15th Punjab Regiment in the middle of April and took over command of the Battalion.

Reorganization.

In July, 1929, the Indian Army experienced another of its frequent reorganizations—this time, fortunately, within the Battalion. "B" Company, which had up to now been a rifle company, was henceforth to be a Machine Gun Company, consisting of one platoon of Vickers machine guns, six in number. The title of company was still retained in order to admit of expansion in war. The composition of this company was one section each of Sikhs, Punjabi Muhammadans and Dogras. The surplus Muhammadans in the Battalion were gradually absorbed.

On December 31st, 1929, Colours were presented to the Battalion by His Excellency Sir Frederick Hugh Sykes, P.C., G.C.I.E., G.B.E., K.C.B., C.M.G., Governor of Bombay, and were consecrated by the Right Reverend the Bishop of Bombay, Bishop Ackland. The next day the Colours were blessed by the religious teachers of the Battalion according to the Sikh, Muhammadan and Dogra religions. These Colours were the first official Colours the Battalion had ever received. Mention has previously been made of Colours in 1880, and of the cavalry guidons in 1824, but it is doubtful if these were other than privately purchased. The battle honours of all battalions in the 16th Group were emblazoned on the Colours ; those engagements at which the Battalion were present being noted below with an asterisk :—

Presentation of Colours.

ON THE KING'S COLOUR.

*" La Bassée, 1914."	*" Givenchy, 1914."
*" Ypres, 1915."	" Loos."
" Mediggo."	*" Tigris, 1916."
*" Kut-al-Amara, 1917."	*" Baghdad."
" Narumgombe."	" Nyangao."

ON THE REGIMENTAL COLOUR.

*" Afghanistan, 1878-80."	" Burma, 1885-87."
" Chitral."	" Tirah."
" Punjab Frontier."	" Malakand."

"Afghanistan, 1919."

In the ceremony His Excellency made an address reviewing the history of the Battalion, his concluding words are given below in full :—

" This is a history of which any regiment may be justly proud, and it is a matter of surprise to me to hear that up to to-day you have not possessed Colours. The Colours I have now presented to you comprise the King's Colour and the Regimental Colour. The former is His Imperial Majesty's own personal flag, which it is your duty to guard, and the Regimental Colour is your own emblem embodying the history of this Battalion. The battle honours, emblazoned on these Colours must have a special significance for you, and the fact that these honours are the honours of all of the five battalions of the 16th Punjab Regiment is a reminder to you that your Regiment is not composed of five separate bodies but one body, and that the honour of each battalion should be to you as the honour of your Battalion.

"Colours, as you may know, have always been held by fighting troops as a sacred emblem, and although it is not now necessary or possible for the Colours to accompany the troops in battle, yet the spirit of the Colours and all they mean will, I trust, always remain a sacred emblem.

"It is with every confidence that I have handed these Colours to your custody in the firm belief that you will guard them and in every way prove worthy of the great honour bestowed on you."

In January, 1930, orders were received to the effect that the Battalion was to proceed to Chitral in the autumn. In April the 1st Battalion 6th Rajputana Rifles came to Ahmedabad to relieve the Battalion of its internal security duties, thus allowing all the Indian ranks to proceed on four months' furlough.

Early this year Gandhi's so-called Civil Disobedience campaign was launched against the Government. The Battalion was never called out in aid of the civil power, nor was there any interference with the military, except on one occasion. On this occasion, Captains W. J. Cawthorne and V. P. Northam were purchasing liquor for the Battalion to take up to Chitral, when two followers of Gandhi lay down in front of and behind their motor-car. The car was thus rendered immobile until the police were summoned. All were pleased to hear, later, that these two men passed the next six months in jail.

In May, Major N. H. H. Ralston was appointed Commandant of the 10th Battalion, and left immediately for Multan. He had served continuously with the Battalion for twenty-four years, and his absence was greatly felt. Major A. H. N. Gatherer, M.C., was appointed Second-in-Command in his stead.

By August 20th the Battalion had once more assembled. There remained only ten days in which to train the men for marching, inoculate them, and pack up their baggage. The amount of work involved in the latter may be gauged by the fact that there were some 2,100 packages to be made up, each of which had to weigh exactly one maund. On the 30th, however, all was ready and the Battalion left by troop train under command of Major J. C. D. Mullaly, arriving at Dargai on September 3rd. The itinerary of the march to Chitral is as follows:

March to Chitral.

Date.			*From*	*To*	*Miles.*
September	5th	...	Dargai	Khar	13
,,	6th	...	Khar	Chakdara	10
,,	7th	...	Chakdara	Serai	12
,,	8th	...	Serai	Sado	12
,,	9th	...	Sado	Robat	12
,,	10th	...	Robat	Warai	11
,,	11th	...	Warai	Darora	12
,,	12th	...	Darora	Dir	13
,,	13th	...	Halt at Dir		—
,,	14th	...	Dir	Mirga	8
,,	15th	...	Mirga	Ziarat	9 (over the Laori Pass)
,,	16th	...	Ziarat	Nagar	11
,,	17th	...	Nagar	Drosh	7

At Khar and at Chakdara the relief column was rationed by aeroplanes, this being the first time that this method of rationing had been employed in India. The rations were attached to parachutes, the majority of which fell within four hundred yards of the camp. In the previous years it had been customary for a whole brigade to act as escort to the Chitral Reliefs. This year, however, the troops could not be spared owing to political disturbances in the Peshawar District, and it was therefore decided to rely entirely on the Nawab of Dir to protect the column. From Chakdara to Dir the Nawab employed every able-bodied man from the near-by villages for this purpose. At night one could see as many as a thousand fires lighting up the hills surrounding the camp, each fire denoting a small picquet of the Nawab's protective troops.

For the first time in the history of the Chitral Reliefs, Army mule cart transport was used as far north as Dir. Their use was a mixed blessing, as some of the gradients of the road were so steep that the whole Battalion was frequently employed helping the carts up the hill. During the march to Darora the advanced guard reached camp at noon, but the last of the carts did not arrive till 6 p.m.

The total casualties during the march amounted to four men sick. The men were carrying, in addition to their rifles and equipment, one hundred rounds of ammunition, waterproof capes and packs—a total weight of fifty-four pounds. In addition to this the men were not in training after their four months' furlough. Hence the Battalion's march can be considered as a very fine performance. In Chitral the Battalion relieved the 4th Battalion 6th Rajputana Rifles. The Battalion was stationed at Kila Drosh with one company on detachment at Fort Chitral. This company was relieved every four months

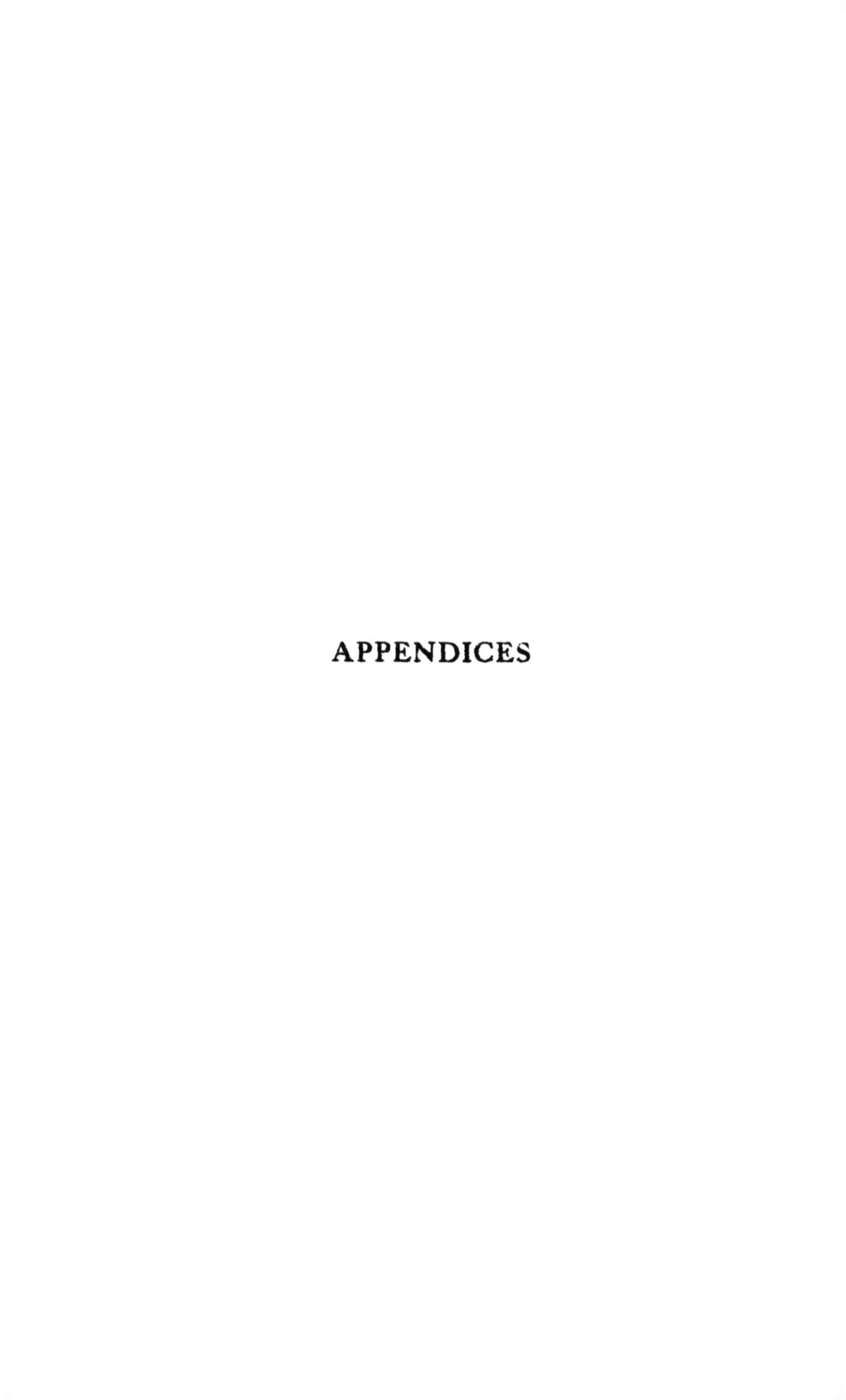

APPENDICES

APPENDIX I

ROLL OF HONOUR, 9TH BHOPAL INFANTRY

List of British Officers Died of Wounds, Disease and Killed in Action during the Great War.

Rank and Name.	*Date of Casualty.*	*Remarks.*
Captain R. F. Clarke	10-3-15	Killed in action. Attached from 1/39th Garhwalis.
Lieut.-Colonel H. L. Anderson	28-10-14	Killed in action.
Captain G. H. W. Mortimer ...	29-11-14	Killed in action. Attached from 10th Jats.
Captain G. E. Cavendish ...	22-12-14	Killed in action. Attached from 97th Infantry.
Captain L. J. Jones	28-10-14	Killed in action.
Lieutenant H. W. Wade ...	28-10-14	Killed in action.
Captain H. E. Etlenger ...	27-4-15	Died of wounds.
Captain E. H. F. Apthorpe ...	14-11-14	Died of wounds. Attached from 90th Punjabis.
Major G. A. Jamieson	13-1-16	Died of wounds.
Lieut.-Colonel F. W. Thomas ...	26-1-16	Killed in action.
Lieutenant D. F. Hubert ...	14-3-17	Killed in action.
Captain R. D'A. S. Banks ...	21-4-17	Killed in action.
Major G. B. C. Irvine	15-5-17	Killed in action.

List of Indian Officers Died of Wounds or Disease and Killed in Action during the Great War.

Rank and Name.	*Date of Casualty.*	*Remarks.*
Subedar Partab Singh	28-10-14	Killed in action.
Subedar Baijnath Singh ...	28-10-14	Killed in action.
Subedar Ram Lal Dube ...	28-10-14	Killed in action.
Jemadar Sidh Nath Missir ...	28-10-14	Killed in action.
Subedar Faiz Ali Khan ...	23-11-14	Killed in action.
Jemadar Mulloo Singh	23-11-14	Killed in action.
Jemadar Mirsa Mustaq Ali ...	23-11-14	Killed in action.
Jemadar Ramadhin Tewari ...	23-11-14	Killed in action. Attached from 89th Punjabis.
Jemadar Ganga Narain Sukul...	13-4-16	Killed in action.
Jemadar Sher Mohammed ...	9-7-16	Killed in action. Attached from 5th Light Infantry.
Jemadar Hussain Ali	21-4-17	Killed in action.

LIST OF INDIAN OTHER RANKS DIED OF WOUNDS, DISEASE AND KILLED IN ACTION DURING THE GREAT WAR.

Regtl. No.	*Rank and Name.*		*Date of Casualty.*	*Remarks.*
2363	Havildar Sheoparshad Dube	...	28-10-14	Killed in action.
3614	Drummer Kehar Singh ...	...	28-10-14	„ „
3151	Sepoy Gurbakhsh Singh	...	28-10-14	„ „
3385	Sepoy Uttam Singh ...	...	28-10-14	„ „
2443	Sepoy Sundar Singh ...	...	28-10-14	„ „
3408	Sepoy Tota Singh ...	...	28-10-14	„ „
1948	Sepoy Bagga Singh ...	...	28-10-14	„ „
3440	Sepoy Hazara Singh ...	...	28-10-14	„ „
3668	Sepoy Abdul Ghani Khan	...	28-10-14	„ „
3597	Sepoy Rahmat Ullah Khan	...	28-10-14	„ „
3496	Sepoy Parsan Singh ...	...	28-10-14	„ „
3442	Sepoy Bahan Singh ...	...	7-11-14	„ „
3115	Sepoy Barnam Singh ...	...	7-11-14	„ „
3376	Sepoy Ram Singh ...	...	7-11-14	„ „
3417	Sepoy Drig Pal Ditchit ...	...	7-11-14	„ „
3116	Sepoy Sahdeo Parsad Tewari	...	7-11-14	„ „
2701	Havildar Sheodarshan Dube	...	8-11-14	„ „
2366	Sepoy Prag Datt Dube ...	...	8-11-14	„ „
3498	Sepoy Mata Parsad Awasthi	...	8-11-14	„ „
3105	Sepoy Ram Singh ...	...	28-10-14	„ „
2868	L/Naik Dasratdin Upadhya	...	28-10-14	„ „
3587	Sepoy Chainchal Singh ...	...	28-10-14	„ „
3650	Sepoy Lakha Singh ...	...	28-10-14	„ „
3095	Sepoy Sheoparshad Upadhya	...	28-10-14	„ „
2344	Havildar Daya Singh ...	...	28-10-14	„ „
2407	Colour/Havildar Kartar Singh	...	23-11-14	„ „
2561	Naik Karam Ali Khan ...	...	23-11-14	„ „
3713	Sepoy Mall Singh ...	...	23-11-14	„ „
3272	Sepoy Dindar Khan ...	...	23-11-14	„ „
3078	Sepoy Shivraj Singh ...	...	23-11-14	„ „
3481	Sepoy Tulsi Ram Pande	...	23-11-14	„ „
2383	Sepoy Brahmadin Upadhya	...	23-11-14	„ „
3397	Sepoy Laltan Singh ...	...	23-11-14	„ „
3393	Sepoy Hansraj Singh ...	...	23-11-14	„ „
3079	Sepoy Debi Singh ...	...	23-11-14	„ „
2790	Sepoy Mahanand Sukul	...	23-11-14	„ „
2320	Sepoy Badal Tiwari ...	...	23-11-14	„ „
2634	Sepoy Badri Chaube ...	...	23-11-14	„ „
3578	Sepoy Methura Pande Missir	...	23-11-14	„ „
3661	Sepoy Mani Lal Tiwari ...	...	23-11-14	„ „
3516	Sepoy Bishan Singh ...	...	23-11-14	„ „
3705	Sepoy Karam Illahi Khan	...	23-11-14	„ „
2679	Sepoy Imam Uddin ...	...	21-12-14	„ „
3359	L./Naik Naratha Singh ...	...	28-10-14	„ „
2609	Sepoy Ram Singh ...	...	28-10-14	„ „
3672	Sepoy Mehar Singh ...	...	28-10-14	„ „
3432	Sepoy Phuman Singh ...	...	28-10-14	„ „
3476	Sepoy Dalip Singh ...	...	28-10-14	„ „
2918	Havildar Ram Sharak Tiwari	...	28-10-14	„ „
2615	Drummer Nizam Uddin	...	28-10-14	„ „
3410	Sepoy Umrao Ali Khan	...	28-10-14	„ „
3633	Sepoy Abdul Rahman Khan	...	28-10-14	„ „
2707	Sepoy Bisresar Chaube ...	...	28-10-14	„ „
3610	Sepoy Misrilal Dube ...	...	28-10-14	„ „

Regtl. No.	Rank and Name.	Date of Casualty.	Remarks.
3276	Naik Randhir Singh	28-10-14	Killed in action.
3729	Sepoy Kanhaiya Pande	19-5-15	,, ,,
3289	Sepoy Asghar Ali Khan ...	23-11-14	,, ,,
3605	Sepoy Niaz Ali	28-10-14	,, ,,
2573	Sepoy Bathawal Khan	28-10-14	,, ,,
2559	Sepoy Asghar Khan	28-10-14	,, ,,
3336	Sepoy Kale Khan	28-10-14	,, ,,
3608	Sepoy Brig Mohan Singh ...	28-10-14	,, ,,
3726	Sepoy Sanawal Singh	28-10-14	,, ,,
2327	Sepoy Baijnath Sukul	23-11-14	,, ,,
3583	Sepoy Puran Singh	30-10-14	Died of wounds.
3271	L./Naik Mazhar Ali	25-11-14	,, ,,
3609	Sepoy Bhup Singh	4-12-14	,, ,,
3658	Sepoy Raghu Singh	5-1-15	Died of disease.
1375	Sepoy Phugwandin Sukul ...	12-4-15	,, ,,
3067	Sepoy Manna Tiwari	20-4-15	,, ,,
3041	Naik Niaz Mohd Khan	25-7-15	,, ,,
3703	Sepoy Maksud Khan	17-7-15	,, ,,
3629	Sepoy Mathura Singh	6-6-19	Prisoner of war. Died after released.
2198	Sepoy Rachpal Singh	31-1-15	Died whilst prisoner of war.
2140	Sepoy Sheoraj Singh	22-4-15	,, ,,
2445	Sepoy Ram Charan Singh ...	24-4-15	,, ,,
2713	Sepoy Mangal Singh	21-4-15	,, ,,
3471	Sepoy Bhagwat Dube	8-5-15	,, ,,
3652	Sepoy Sohan Singh	5-7-15	,, ,,
3642	Sepoy Bhulai Singh	25-7-15	,, ,,
2146	Sepoy Chandarpal Singh ...	2-8-15	,, ,,
3480	Sepoy Bachai Singh	4-8-15	,, ,,
3099	Sepoy Raghubir Singh ...	9-9-15	,, ,,
2569	Havildar Gokul Singh	3-9-15	,, ,,
2469	Sepoy Mata Din Singh	22-9-15	,, ,,
3390	Sepoy Ram Samujh Tiwari ...	17-7-15	,, ,,
3611	Sepoy Har Lal Missir	22-7-15	,, ,,
3681	Sepoy Gainda Singh	28-10-15	,, ,,
2588	Sepoy Sheobarat Singh	19-1-16	,, ,,
3439	Sepoy Bhagat Singh	5-12-15	,, ,,
3364	Sepoy Darsan Singh	19-2-16	,, ,,
3625	Sepoy Ram Nath Singh ...	5-3-16	,, ,,
3666	Sepoy Naresh Singh	12-3-16	,, ,,
3763	L./Naik Thakur Singh	7-2-16	,, ,,
2597	Havildar Ram Bharose Missir ...	24-5-16	,, ,,
3514	Sepoy Lalta Singh ...	Date unknown	,, ,,
3665	Havildar Pahalwan Singh ...	2-7-16	,, ,,
2896	Havildar Bhagwat Pande ...	3-11-15	,, ,,
3491	Havildar Ishawar Singh ...	10-7-15	,, ,,
3601	Havildar Harnam Singh ...	30-7-16	,, ,,
3300	Sepoy Pattu Singh	13-9-16	,, ,,
1950	Sepoy Ashraf Khan	1-9-16	,, ,,
2684	Sepoy Ram Singh ...	Date unknown	,, ,,
2739	Sepoy Ram Lal Singh	22-10-16	,, ,,
3696	Sepoy Fateh Singh	16-12-16	,, ,,
3644	Sepoy Beni Madho Singh ...	18-12-16	,, ,,
3031	Naik Sheoram Singh	23-1-17	,, ,,
3522	Sepoy Debi Din Singh	24-8-16	,, ,,

Regtl. No.	Rank and Name.	Date of Casualty.	Remarks.
3255	Sepoy Ramasre Singh	21-8-16	Died whilst prisoner of war.
2862	Sepoy Mahipal Singh	4-3-17	" "
2806	Sepoy Sarop Singh	11-3-17	" "
3699	Sepoy Babu Singh	28-3-17	" "
1993	Sepoy Magha Singh	29-5-17	" "
3685	Sepoy Bhaironath Missir ...	23-12-17	" "
2782	Sepoy Debi Dayal Singh ...	7-2-18	" "
3024	Sepoy Raghunath Singh ...	28-12-17	" "
3517	Sepoy Chanan Singh	23-3-18	" "
3606	Sepoy Dulle Khan	17-3-18	" "
3784	Sepoy Sher Singh	14-12-16	" "
3344	Sepoy Ishar Singh (Tehar) ...	28-3-18	" "
2649	Sepoy Hari Singh	8-5-17	" "
3087	Sepoy Ram Kumar Sukal ...	11-2-15	" "
3431	Sepoy Gujjar Singh	25-9-17	" "
3593	Sepoy Jiwan Singh	28-4-17	" "
2337	Havildar Hari Singh	18-12-18	Prisoner of war ; died after release
2095	Havildar Mahabir Singh ...	21-12-18	" "
2508	Sepoy Babu Singh	23-1-19	" "
3741	Sepoy Ram Singh	9-12-18	" "
4845	Sepoy Umrao Singh	14-3-17	Killed in action.
4677	Sepoy Nand Bahadur	14-3-17	" "
4202	Sepoy Durjan Singh	14-3-17	" "
4903	Sepoy Bhure Khan	14-3-17	" "
4188	Sepoy Ghulam Qadir	14-3-17	" "
4181	Sepoy Mala Singh	14-3-17	" "
2616	Sepoy Mana Singh	14-3-17	" "
3532	Havildar Ahmed Din	21-4-17	" "
4596	Havildar Nand Lal	21-4-17	" "
3293	L./Naik Kehar Singh	21-4-17	" "
3326	L./Naik Abdullah	21-4-17	" "
3222	Sepoy Imam Uddin	21-4-17	" "
3896	Sepoy Lal Singh	21-4-17	" "
3996	Sepoy Jalal Khan	21-4-17	" "
4018	Sepoy Nadir Ali	21-4-17	" "
4059	Sepoy Lachman Singh	21-4-17	" "
4197	Sepoy Gunga Singh	21-4-17	" "
4298	Sepoy Lachman Singh	21-4-17	" "
4455	Sepoy Musarif Khan	21-4-17	" "
4664	Sepoy Bihari Singh	21-4-17	" "
4707	Sepoy Nazir Ali	21-4-17	" "
4722	Sepoy Haidar Bakhsh	21-4-17	" "
4755	Sepoy Gangan Singh	21-4-17	" "
4784	Sepoy Rahim	21-4-17	" "
4800	Sepoy Prem Singh	21-4-17	" "
4974	Sepoy Bhagwan Singh	21-4-17	" "
3715	Sepoy Salam Uddin	13-1-16	" "
2548	Sepoy Karam Ali Khan ...	13-1-16	" "
3172	Sepoy Murad Ali Khan	13-1-16	" "
3760	Sepoy Sakhawat Khan	13-1-16	" "
3869	Sepoy Suleman Khan	13-1-16	" "
2374	Havildar Dwarka Pande ...	13-1-16	" "
3028	L./Naik Bharosa Singh	13-1-16	" "
2374	Sepoy Hardiyal Singh	13-1-16	" "
3166	Sepoy Bharnon Pande	13-1-16	" "

Regtl. No.	Rank and Name.	Date of Casualty.	Remarks.
4095	Sepoy Harnam Singh	13-1-16	Killed in action.
4035	Sepoy Sultan Ali	7-1-16	,, ,,
3997	Sepoy Mohammed Alam ...	7-1-16	,, ,,
3798	Sepoy Mehar Singh	21-1-16	,, ,,
4185	Sepoy Ram Singh	21-1-16	,, ,,
3761	Sepoy Bharat Singh	21-1-16	,, ,,
3749	Sepoy Imtiaz Khan	21-1-16	,, ,,
3767	Sepoy Bassir Ahmed Khan ...	16-2-16	,, ,,
3934	Sepoy Shamsher Singh	5-3-16	,, ,,
3892	Sepoy Allahyar Khan	10-3-16	,, ,,
2708	Havildar Ramzan Khan ...	12-4-16	,, ,,
2393	Naik Sakhat Singh	12-4-16	,, ,,
2800	Naik Parbhunath Tiwari ...	12-4-16	,, ,,
4132	Sepoy Abdul Rahman	12-4-16	,, ,,
3876	Sepoy Ishaq Mohd Khan ...	18-4-16	,, ,,
4143	Sepoy Satram Singh	18-4-16	,, ,,
2725	Sepoy Matadin Singh	5-6-16	,, ,,
4281	Sepoy Pancham Singh	8-6-16	,, ,,
4410	Sepoy Sarjuparsad Tiwari ...	23-5-16	,, ,,
4245	Sepoy Gungan Singh	14-10-16	,, ,,
4073	Sepoy Raghuraj Singh	15-12-16	,, ,,
4319	Sepoy Dinda Singh	15-12-16	,, ,,
4478	Havildar Basant Parsad Missir	14-3-17	,, ,,
4361	Sepoy Kalka Singh	14-3-17	,, ,,
4359	Sepoy Mitan Singh	14-3-17	,, ,,
4491	Sepoy Deodatt	14-3-17	,, ,,
489	Sepoy Chhotu	21-4-17	,, ,,
3278	Naik Rahmat Ali Khan ...	8-1-16	Died of wounds.
3269	L./Naik Karam Ali	8-1-16	,, ,,
3728	L./Naik Rameshwar Dube ...	16-1-16	,, ,,
2369	L./Naik Balbhadra Singh ...	24-1-16	,, ,,
3341	L./Naik Kuber Sukul	3-3-16	,, ,,
4192	L./Naik Yusif Khan	28-1-16	,, ,,
4161	L./Naik Male Khan	22-3-16	,, ,,
4450	Sepoy Gafoor Khan	16-4-16	,, ,,
3854	Sepoy Labh Singh	19-4-16	,, ,,
4125	Sepoy Sultan Hassan Khan ...	22-4-16	,, ,,
3366	Havildar Rur Singh	22-5-16	,, ,,
4563	Sepoy Ram Charan Tiwari ...	3-6-16	,, ,,
4231	Sepoy Harchand Singh	9-6-16	,, ,,
4691	Sepoy Tarloki Singh	12-12-16	,, ,,
4676	Sepoy Ram Nath Singh ...	27-2-17	,, ,,
4160	Sepoy Chhote Khan	17-3-17	,, ,,
4934	Sepoy Sheoratan Singh	15-3-17	,, ,,
3281	Sepoy Sadiq Khan	15-3-17	,, ,,
4628	Sepoy Amin Lal	15-3-17	,, ,,
3637	Sepoy Partab Singh	22-4-17	,, ,,
3582	Sepoy Ujagar Singh	16-2-17	,, ,,
3871	Sepoy Bashir Mohd Khan ...	27-12-15	Died of disease.
3911	Sepoy Gauri Singh	23-1-16	,, ,,
3472	Sepoy Bachhu Singh	14-2-16	,, ,,
3956	Sepoy Siripal Singh	22-2-16	,, ,,
3913	Sepoy Rai Singh	16-1-16	,, ,,
2276	Sepoy Harnam Singh	16-4-16	,, ,,
3802	Sepoy Ramadhar Singh ...	2-8-16	,, ,,
2385	Havildar Ratan Singh	2-9-16	,, ,,
4036	Sepoy Rahmat Khan	27-1-16	,, ,,

Regtl. No.	*Rank and Name.*	*Date of Casualty.*	*Remarks.*
3106	Sepoy Sheodhar Missir	28-8-16	Died of disease.
3133	Sepoy Sheolal Singh	4-10-16	" "
2505	Naik Hakim Ali Khan	4-10-16	" "
3109	Sepoy Mahesar Tiwari	3-12-16	" "
3781	L./Naik Harkaran Singh ...	23-12-16	" "
4559	L./Naik Pranshankar Missir ...	27-12-16	" "
3434	Sepoy Ram Singh	17-12-16	" "
3690	Sepoy Niamat Khan	27-1-17	" "
1194	Naik Panchhan Singh	22-12-16	" "
4665	Sepoy Balwant Singh	21-2-17	" "
4584	Sepoy Gulsher Khan	19-2-17	" "
4858	Sepoy Mahbub Ali	28-2-17	" "
4718	Sepoy Satnarain Pande	10-3-17	" "
3742	Sepoy Harnam Singh	16-3-17	" "
272	Sepoy Ganda Singh	4-4-17	" "
271	Sepoy Mam Chand	13-5-17	" "
4963	Sepoy Chandan Singh	7-6-17	" "
3867	L./Naik Kalesh Singh	6-10-17	" "
324	Sepoy Hardayal	7-11-17	" "
66	Sepoy Nand Ram	2-12-17	" "
455	Sepoy Bansgopal Singh	30-12-17	" "
4993	L./Naik Karam Bakhsh ...	15-11-17	" "
3015	Sepoy Duri Singh	20-2-18	" "
3136	L./Naik Taj Mohammed Khan	18-2-18	" "
3591	Sepoy Tara Singh	2-12-17	" "
430	Sepoy Dada Singh	22-4-18	" "
3771	Sepoy Khair Uddin Khan ...	2-4-18	" "
1993	Sepoy Ram Singh	28-5-18	" "
160	Sepoy Hardewa	7-8-18	" "
4690	Sepoy Mohari Tiwari	5-1-19	" "
4771	Sepoy Janki Parsad Aganhotri	16-1-19	" "
1081	Sepoy Badri Singh	18-1-19	" "
405	Naik Mansa Ram	25-4-19	" "
	Sepoy Ramdin Ramavtal ...	29-3-16	Died whilst prisoner of war.
9848	Naik Fazar Ali	13-12-18	Died of disease.

List of Followers Died of Wounds or Disease and Killed in Action during the Great War.

Rank and Name.	*Date of Casualty.*	*Remarks.*
Sweeper Chunni	29-11-14	Died of disease.
Cook Nanuha	30-11-14	" "
Sweeper Mirchi	1-12-14	" "
Sweeper Chandgi	1-12-17	" "
Cook Jaman	15-2-15	" "
Cook Sheikh Juman	15-2-15	" "
Cook Phul Parsad	18-2-15	" "
Cook Sheo Narain Tewari	26-4-15	Killed in action.
Cook Ganga Parsad	22-7-15	Died of disease.
Cook Milkanath Upadhiya	10-5-16	" "
Cook Ralla Singh	14-2-17	Died of wounds.

APPENDIX II

HONOURS AND AWARDS, 1914-1919

VICTORIA CROSS.

3398 SEPOY CHATTA SINGH.

In Mesopotamia on January 21st, 1916. For the most conspicuous bravery and devotion to duty in leaving cover to assist his Officer Commanding who was lying wounded and helpless in the open. He bound up the officer's wound and then dug cover for him with his entrenching tool, being exposed all the time to very heavy rifle fire. For five hours until nightfall he remained beside the wounded officer, shielding him with his own body on the exposed side. He then, under cover of darkness, went back for assistance and brought the officer into safety.

(*Note.*—Lieutenant-Colonel F. W. Thomas was the officer in question and shortly afterwards died from his wounds.)

DISTINGUISHED SERVICE ORDER.

CAPTAIN H. H. SMITH.

MILITARY CROSS.

CAPTAIN G. D. MARTIN.
LIEUTENANT F. C. ROBERTS.
LIEUTENANT E. A. STEAD.
CAPTAIN M. DAS, I.M.S.

INDIAN ORDER OF MERIT (1ST CLASS).

JEMADAR JAI LAL.

For conspicuous gallantry, resource, and devotion to duty in action on April 21st, 1917, in Mesopotamia. The Regiment having suffered heavy casualties and some of the men having begun to withdraw, this Indian officer, on his own initiative, recalled them, led them forward in the face of severe fire, and retook some of the ground lost.

INDIAN ORDER OF MERIT (2ND CLASS).

SUBEDAR ABAIDATT SINGH.

For conspicuous gallantry and resource in action on April 21st, 1916, in Mesopotamia, when on his own initiative he led his men forward in face of severe gun-fire and retook some lost ground. He handled his men with great ability and by his disregard of personal danger set a fine example of cool daring and devotion to duty.

3943 SEPOY MUGLI KHAN.

For conspicuous gallantry and coolness on April 12th, 1916, in Mesopotamia, when the water in the Suwaikiyeh Marsh was blown into the forward trenches filling them rapidly and forcing the garrison to vacate them. The enemy took advantage of this opportunity to pour in a heavy shell and machine-gun fire. On his own initiative, in full view of the enemy, regardless of personal risk, he erected a barricade in the trench with the assistance of a comrade, to enable two badly wounded men to be got away. But for this act these wounded men would have been drowned.

3266 SEPOY MAHMUD ALI KHAN.

For conspicuous gallantry and coolness on April 12th, 1916, in Mesopotamia. When water from the Suwaikiyeh Marsh was blown into the forward trenches, filling them rapidly and forcing the garrison to evacuate them, the enemy took advantage of this opportunity to pour in a heavy shell and machine-gun fire. On his own initiative, in full view of the enemy, regardless of personal risk, he erected a barricade in the trench with the assistance of a comrade, to enable two badly wounded men to be evacuated. But for this act these wounded men would have been drowned.

INDIAN DISTINGUISHED SERVICE MEDAL.

2609 SEPOY ABDUL LATIF.

For continuous gallantry while serving with the Battalion in France.

2867 NAIK ANGAD PANDE.

For particular gallantry and coolness in the field. In France, on May 8th, 1915, when as a signaller, finding the telephone cable broken, he carried a message under heavy shrapnel fire up the La Bassee Road and delivered it to a British officer at Port Arthur. On his way back he mended the cable and re-established communication.

4132 HAVILDAR ISHAR SINGH.

2708 HAVILDAR RAMZAN KHAN.

Action of Shaikh Saad, January 7th-8th, 1916. These men formed part of the machine-gun detachment on January 7th, and after the machine-gun officer and eleven men had been wounded, Havildars Ishar Singh and Ramzan Khan, with four men, brought their guns into the firing line at 4 p.m. under heavy rifle fire and worked the guns with good effect. The whole party showed great coolness and daring.

342 SEPOY SHEO CHAND.

For marked gallantry in action at Sannaiyat, on 17th February, 1917. When the machine guns were withdrawn, he brought up the rear of his party. He saw one of the enemy in the trenches and went for him but he ran away. Sepoy Sheo Chand however chased and bayoneted him and brought him back a prisoner.

JEMADAR SHER MOHAMMED KHAN.

For gallant and distinguished service.

3433 LANCE-NAIK MAIMA SINGH.

For consistent good work and devotion to duty in the field (Mesopotamia) since the outbreak of the war. He has been twice wounded.

69 SEPOY TEJA SINGH.

For gallantry in action. During a withdrawal a wounded Indian officer could not move and had been left behind and would have been captured had not this Sepoy dashed forward under heavy fire and carried him back to a place of safety some 150 yards in rear.

3142 LANCE-NAIK SARJU MISSIR.

For gallantry in action. During a withdrawal a wounded Indian officer who could not move and had been left behind and would have been captured had not this N.C.O. dashed forward under heavy fire and carried him back to a place of safety some 100 yards in rear.

2747 SEPOY UMRAO SINGH.
No details.

SUBEDAR SHEODARSHAN TEWARI.

This officer was continually on active service from August, 1914, to March, 1919. He saw the early fighting in France. On all occasions he displayed great gallantry in the field and did his work thoroughly and conscientiously during periods of rest. The comparative freedom from caste prejudices of Brahmins in the Battalion is attributed in a large measure to his influence.

SUBEDAR-MAJOR BHURE SINGH.

At Neuve Chapelle on October 28th, 1914. For gallantry in holding on to his portion of the trench under difficult circumstances when the remainder of the line had gone. Under very heavy rifle and artillery fire he showed an example of coolness and daring. It was mainly due to this Indian officer's fine example that the portion of the line entrusted him remained intact.

2203 HAVILDAR AMAR SINGH.

At Neuve Chapelle on October 28th, 1914. This N.C.O. throughout the day showed conspicuous gallantry under a heavy rifle fire and artillery fire. He led his section with ability and skill during the attack. At one time he became isolated but continued to hold the ground gained till dark and then only withdrew when ordered to do so by his company commander.

THE ORDER OF BRITISH INDIA (2ND CLASS).

SUBEDAR GOVIND SINGH.

For devotion to duty in France, Egypt and Mesopotamia since he left India with the Battalion in August, 1914. He led his platoon very gallantly on every occasion. Wounded in the thigh in November, 1914, he soon returned to the Battalion and has since never gone sick, though on occasions he has suffered from fever or other complaints. On more than one occasion he has had to command his double company and has done it well.

MERITORIOUS SERVICE MEDAL.

3250 COLOUR-HAVILDAR ALLAH DAD KHAN.

For meritorious service and devotion to duty while serving with the Mesopotamia Expeditionary Force.

2745 COLOUR-HAVILDAR SURAJ PRASAD MISSIR.

For meritorious service and devotion to duty while serving with the Mesopotamia Expeditionary Force.

3159 HAVILDAR SHEO SAHAI DUBE.

For meritorious service and devotion to duty while serving with the Mesopotamia Expeditionary Force.

2069 NAIK ABDUL LATIF.

For meritorious service and devotion to duty while serving with the Mesopotamia Expeditionary Force.

2546 COLOUR-HAVILDAR ALLADIN KHAN.

For meritorious service and devotion to duty while serving with the Mesopotamia Expeditionary Force.

3386 HAVILDAR INDAR SINGH.

For meritorious service and devotion to duty while serving with the Mesopotamia Expeditionary Force.

3743 HAVILDAR ARJAN SINGH.

For meritorious service and devotion to duty while serving with the Mesopotamia Expeditionary Force.

2192 HAVILDAR SHEIKH WAHID.

For meritorious service and devotion to duty while serving with the Mesopotamia Expeditionary Force.

BREVET LIEUTENANT-COLONEL.

MAJOR H. H. SMITH.
MAJOR G. D. MARTIN.

BREVET MAJOR.

CAPTAIN C. H. JARDINE (96th Infantry, attached).

ALLIED DECORATIONS.

SERBIAN WHITE EAGLE (5TH CLASS).

CAPTAIN G. D. MARTIN.

RUSSIAN ORDER OF SAINT GEORGE (2ND CLASS).

SUBEDAR NAZIR KHAN.
3532 NAIK AHMED DIN.

ROUMANIAN BARBATIE CREDINTA (3RD CLASS).

3107 NAIK KAMPTA SINGH.

SERBIAN KARAGEORGE (2ND CLASS) (WITH SWORDS).

3194 SEPOY UMED KHAN.
4842 SEPOY HARNAM SINGH.

APPENDIX III

SUCCESSION ROLL OF COMMANDING OFFICERS 1824 TO 1929.

Rank at the Time of assuming Command.	*Name.*	*Commanded From*	*To*
Captain	J. Johnson	1824	?
Captain	Winfield	1835	1838
Captain	Riddel	1838	1839
Captain	J. E. Landers...	1840	1849
Major	Thomson	1850	1854
Colonel	J. T. Travers, V.C.	1854	1860
Colonel	Hamilton-Forbes	1860	1879
Lieutenant-Colonel	J. D. Hall	1880	1885
Colonel	G. R. Peart	1886	1895
Major	E. S. Masters	1895	1896
Lieutenant-Colonel	G. A. Collins	1896	1899
Lieutenant-Colonel	G. H. J. Moore	1900	1906
Lieutenant-Colonel	C. A. Brown	1906	1910
Lieutenant-Colonel	C. F. Dobbie	1910	1915
*	* *	*	*
Lieutenant-Colonel	H. H. Smith, D.S.O.... ...	1918	1925
Lieutenant-Colonel	R. W. Gaskell	1925	1929
Lieutenant-Colonel	G. D. Martin, M.C.	1929	1929
Lieutenant-Colonel	C. N. Steel	1929	—

Note.—During the War no permanent Commandants were appointed.

APPENDIX

ROLL OF BRITISH OFFICERS WHO SERVED

Date of Joining.	*Rank on Joining.*	*Rank attained in Battalion.*	*Name.*
1824	Captain	— ...	J. Johnson ... ...
1835	Captain	— ...	Winfield ... ...
1838	Captain	— ...	Riddel ... ...
1840	Captain	Lieutenant-Colonel	J. E. Landers ... ...
1847	Lieutenant ...	— ...	Trevelion ... ...
1847	Captain	Colonel	J. T. Travers, V.C., C.B.
1847	Assistant-Surgeon	—	Braider ... ...
1850	Major	— ...	Thomson ... ...
1854	Lieutenant ...	— ...	A. C. Lilly ... ...
1854	Captain	— ...	F. L. Magniac ... ...
1858	Captain	— ...	Fuller ... ...
1858	Captain	— ...	C. P. Roberts ... ...
1859	Captain	— ...	Gordon Cumming ...
25-4-59	Major	— ...	A. L. McMillin ...
10-6-59	Captain	— ...	J. Peyton ... ...
25-4-59	Lieutenant ...	— ...	E. Temple ... ...
25-4-59	Assistant-Surgeon	— ...	C. Thomson ... ...
25-4-59	Lieutenant ...	Lieutenant-Colonel	R. C. Cross ... ...
1-5-60	Major	Colonel	L. Hamilton-Forbes ...
1861	Captain	— ...	E. W. Dun ... ...
1865	Lieutenant ...	— ...	Shoolbridge ... ...
22-5-66	Lieutenant ...	Colonel ...	G. R. Peart ... ...
1869	Lieutenant-Colonel	— ...	Duseley ... ...
1870	Captain	— ...	Alexander ... ...
1870	Captain	— ...	F. D. Bignell ... ...
28-5-72	Captain	— ...	Allen ... ...
1870	Surgeon	— ...	F. C. E. Devine ...
16-5-72	Captain	Lieutenant-Colonel	C. Ransford ... ...
25-11-78	Lieutenant ...	Major ...	E. S. Masters ... ...
1878	Lieutenant ...	— ...	W. J. Orr ... ...
1878	Surgeon	— ...	J. L. Corbett ... ...
1-4-79	Colonel	Colonel ...	H. M. Wemyss ...
1879	Lieutenant ...	— ...	Dennys ... ...
1880	Lieutenant-Colonel	Brevet-Colonel ...	J. D. Hall ... ...
1881	Surgeon	Surgeon, Lieutenant-Colonel	A. H. C. Dane ... ...
1885	Lieutenant-Colonel	— ...	J. Miller ... ...
1886	Major	— ...	Jasper Burn ... ...
1886	Lieutenant ...	— ...	Watson ... ...

IV

WITH THE BATTALION, 1818—1914 AND 1922—1930.

Non-effective. *Cause.*	*Date.*	*Remarks.*
No record ...	— ...	—
Retired ...	1838 ...	Commanded Contingent, 1835-1838.
No record ...	1839 ...	Commanded Contingent, 1838-1839.
Retired ...	1849 ...	Commanded Contingent, 1840-1849.
— ...	— ...	First recorded Adjutant.
Transferred ...	May, 1860 ...	Adjutant. First recorded Second-in-Command. Commanded Contingent during Mutiny period. First Commandant of reorganized Bhopal Levy, 1854-1860.
— ...	— ...	Medical Officer.
No record ...	1854 ...	Commanded Contingent, 1850-1854.
— ...	1857 ...	Adjutant.
No record ...	— ...	Second-in-Command.
— ...	— ...	Commanded Artillery of the Contingent during Mutiny.
— ...	— ...	Relieved Captain Fuller in command of artillery of Contingent.
Relieved ...	— ...	Temporarily in charge of remnant of Contingent after the Mutiny.
Relieved ...	10-6-59 ...	Temporary Commanding Officer.
Rejoined own unit ...	March, 1860	Officiating Commanding Officer during raising of Bhopal Levy.
— ...	— ...	First Adjutant of Bhopal Levy.
— ...	— ...	First Medical Officer of Bhopal Levy.
Retired ...	1870 ...	First Second-in-Command of Bhopal Levy.
Appointed Brigade Commander.	1879 ...	Commandant, Bhopal Levy 1860-1879. Commandant during Afghan War, 1878.
— ...	1862 ...	Officiating Commandant.
No record ...	— ...	—
Retired ...	1895 ...	Commandant, 1886-1895.
— ...	1870 ...	—
— ...	— ...	—
— ...	— ...	—
— ...	1880 ...	Medical Officer.
— ...	1871 ...	Medical Officer.
Retired ...	1894 ...	—
Died ...	1896 ...	Adjutant, 1880-1885. Commandant, 1895. Served in Afghan War, 1878, with the Battalion.
— ...	1879 ...	Served in Afghan War, 1878, with the Battalion.
— ...	1879 ...	Medical Officer with the Battalion during Afghan War, 1878-1879.
— ...	1879 ...	Officiating Commandant, Afghan War, 1879.
— ...	1879(?) ...	—
Retired ...	1885 ...	Commandant, 1880-1885.
— ...	1902 ...	Medical Officer.
Retired ...	1886 ...	Commandant, 1885-1886.
— ...	— ...	—
— ...	— ...	—

Date of Joining.	*Rank on Joining.*	*Rank attained in Battalion.*	*Name.*
1886	Lieutenant ...	— ...	H. L. Goodenough. ...
1887	Lieutenant ...	— ...	C. C. Levinson-Gower.
1890	Lieutenant ...	— ...	J. H. Pollard ... ...
1891	Lieutenant ...	— ...	D. Peart ... ...
1891	Lieutenant ...	— ...	C. B. Thornhill ...
1892	Lieutenant ...	— ...	F. C. L. Waller ...
1892	Lieutenant ...	— ...	C. B. Baldock ... ...
1893	Captain	Lieutenant-Colonel	C. G. J. Sutton-Jones
1893	Lieutenant ...	Major ...	C. C. Jackson ... ...
1894	Lieutenant ...	Lieutenant ...	S. R. Davidson ...
1895	Lieutenant ...	— ...	G. V. Holmes ... ...
1895	Captain	— ...	C. Hutton Dawson ...
1896	Lieutenant-Colonel	— ...	G. A. Collins ... ...
20-11-96	Captain	Major ...	B. P. S. Rooke ...
12-11-96	Captain	Captain	E. T. Carwithen ...
23-1-97	Major	Major ...	Poingdestre ... ...
1897	Lieutenant ...	Lieutenant-Colonel	F. W. Thomas ...
1-12-97	Lieutenant ...	Lieutenant-Colonel	H. L. Anderson ...
1898	Captain	Captain	Malcolm Moore ...
3-12-00	Lieutenant ...	Captain	T. E. M. Lane ... ...
1900	Lieutenant-Colonel	Lieutenant-Colonel	G. H. J. Moore ...
26-8-03	Lieutenant ...	Lieutenant ...	W. K. Rollo ... ...
4-10-03	Lieutenant ...	Lieutenant-Colonel	R. W. Gaskell
10-12-03	Lieutenant ...	Lieutenant-Colonel	G. D. Martin, M.C. ...
18-4-00	Lieutenant ...	Major ...	L. J. Jones ... ...
5-3-03	Major	Major	H. Comins ... ...
1903	Lieutenant-Colonel	Lieutenant-Colonel	P. A. Weir ... ...
22-1-04	Lieutenant ...	Lieutenant ...	J. R. Tyrell ... ...
4-5-04	Captain	Captain	J. W. Grant ... ...
1-1-05	Lieutenant ...	Lieutenant ...	W. A. T. Ferris ...
26-3-05	Major	Lieutenant-Colonel	C. F. Dobbie ... ...
26-5-05	Second-Lieutenant	Lieutenant ...	F. V. Pogson ... ...
1905	Second-Lieutenant	Lieutenant ...	R. E. Harenc ... ...
31-3-05	Second-Lieutenant	Lieutenant ...	A. R. O. Mallock ...
10-3-05	Lieutenant ...	Colonel ...	H. H. Smith, D.S.O. ...
14-4-06	Major	Lieutenant-Colonel	C. A. Brown ... ...
18-3-06	Lieutenant ...	Major	G. B. C. Irvine ...
25-10-04	Lieutenant ...	Captain	R. E. Lloyd ... ...
15-9-05	Lieutenant ...	Lieutenant ...	J. O'Leary ... ...
1-3-06	Lieutenant-Colonel	Lieutenant-Colonel	L. C. H. Stawforth ...
10-8-07	Captain	Captain	B. B. Paymaster ...
10-8-07	Lieutenant ...	Major	N. H. H. Ralston ...
26-10-07	Lieutenant ...	Captain	J. A. Burlton-Bennett
24-8-09	Lieutenant ...	Major ...	E. V. Wills, O.B.E. ...
28-11-10	Second-Lieutenant	Lieutenant ...	A. V. Myles ...
8-4-11	Second-Lieutenant	Captain	R. D'A. S. Banks ...
8-8-11	Captain	Captain	G. J. Husband ...
11-12-11	Lieutenant ...	— ...	J. C. D. Mullaly ...
13-4-12	Captain	Major	G. A. Jamieson ...
21-11-12	Captain	Captain	H. Etlenger ... ...
14-6-12	Major	Honorary Colonel	Mohammed Nasrulla Khan Nawab

Non-effective— Cause.	*Date.*	*Remarks.*
—	1896	—
—	1888	—
—	1896	Adjutant, 1892-1894.
—	1896	—
—	1894	—
—	1892	—
—	1894	—
Died	1900	Commandant, 1899-1900.
Transferred	1912	Adjutant, 1894-1897.
Transferred	1901	—
—	1896	—
—	1897	Second-in-Command.
Retired	1899	Commandant, 1896-1899.
Invalided	1906	—
Transferred	1912	To Civil Employment.
Transferred	1900	Second-in-Command.
Killed in action	11-3-1916	—
Killed in action	27-10-14	Adjutant, 1900-1904.
—	1899	Medical Officer.
Retired	1910	—
Retired	1906	Commandant, 1901-1906.
Transferred	1904	—
Retired	1-2-1929	Commandant, 1925-1929.
Died	21-2-29	Adjutant, 1908-1912 ; Commandant, 1929.
Killed in action	27-10-14	Adjutant, 1904-1908.
Transferred	1906	Second-in-Command. To Supply and Transport Corps.
—	1904	Medical Officer.
—	3-5-04	Medical Officer.
—	1904	Medical Officer.
Transferred	1906	To 31st Punjabis.
Invalided	1915	Commandant, 1910-1915.
Transferred	1910	To Supply and Transport Corps.
Transferred	1906	To 4th Cavalry.
Transferred	1908	To the Deoli Regiment.
Retired	1-2-25	Commandant, 1917-1925.
Retired	22-9-10	Commandant, 1906-1910.
Died of wounds	15-5-17	—
Transferred	1905	Medical Officer.
Transferred	1907	Medical Officer.
Retired	13-4-06	Commandant for one and a half months, 1906.
Transferred	1911	Medical Officer.
Transferred	1-5-30	Adjutant, 1912-1916. Second-in-Command, 1928-1930. To 10th Battalion 16th Punjab Regiment.
Transferred	1917	To Supply and Transport Corps.
Transferred	1925	To 3rd Battalion 16th Punjab Regiment.
Invalided	1914	—
Killed in action	21-4-17	—
Transferred	1918	Medical Officer.
—	—	Serving.
Died of wounds	13-1-1916	—
Died of wounds	27-4-15	—
Invalided	1914	Honorary Colonel, 1918-1924.

Date of Joining.	*Rank on Joining.*	*Rank attained in Battalion.*	*Name.*
5-5-13	Lieutenant ...	Captain	G. Brock ... ...
31-3-13	Second-Lieutenant	Lieutenant ...	H. W. Wade ... ...
8-12-12	Major	Major ...	A. De L. Faunce ...
25-3-14	Second-Lieutenant	Captain	B. W. Browning ...
13-10-14	Second-Lieutenant	— ...	W. R. Moll ... ...

For Appointments during the War see Appendix V.

Date of Joining.	*Rank on Joining.*	*Rank attained in Battalion.*	*Name.*
5-8-16	Second-Lieutenant	— ...	L. H. Rodwell ... ...
21-10-18	Lieutenant ...	Lieutenant ...	P. C. J. Leigh ... ...
21-4-21	Lieutenant ...	— ...	J. O. Steabben... ...
6-1-22	Captain	— ...	W. a'C. Beadon ...
3-7-22	Captain	— ...	A. H. N. Gatherer, M.C.
17-8-22	Second-Lieutenant	— ...	V. P. Northam ...
30-8-22	Captain	Captain	H. E. Eve, M.C. ...
28-11-22	Second-Lieutenant	— ...	J. A. Hubert ... ...
1-1-23	Captain	Captain	J. T. Davies, M.B.E. ...
1-1-23	Captain	— ...	W. J. Cawthorn ...
1-1-23	Captain	— ...	S. S. Lavender ...
2-12-23	Lieutenant ...	— ...	E. M. Pyster, M.B.E. ...
18-3-25	Second-Lieutenant	— ...	J. P. Wolfe ... ...
2-10-25	Major	Major	J. S. Ring, O.B.E. ...
6-10-25	Second-Lieutenant	— ...	M. C. B. Steele ...
7-11-28	Second-Lieutenant	— ...	A. C. K. Maunsell ...
26-3-29	Lieutenant ...	Lieutenant ...	S. Goodchild ... ...
18-4-29	Major	— ...	C. N. Steel ... ...
10-7-30	Second-Lieutenant	— ...	J. A. V. Bolam ...

Non-effective— *Cause.*		*Date.*		*Remarks.*
Transferred	...	1914	...	Medical Officer.
Killed in action		28-10-14	...	—
Retired	...	3-7-22	...	Second-in-Command, 1917-1922.
Invalided	...	26-6-23	...	—
—	...	—	...	Adjutant, 1922-1926.—Serving.
—	...	—	...	Adjutant, 1920-1922.—Serving.
Retired	...	26-6-1923	...	Surplus Officers' Scheme.
—	...	—	...	Serving.
—	...	—	...	Adjutant, 1926-1930.—Serving.
—	...	—	...	Second-in-Command, 1930.—Serving.
—	...	—	...	Serving.
Transferred	...	1-6-26	...	To I.A.S.C.
—	...	—	...	Adjutant, 1930.—Serving.
Transferred	...	1-12-24	...	To I.A.S.C.
—	...	—	...	Serving.
—	...	—	...	Serving.
—	...	—	...	Serving.
—	...	—	...	Serving.
Transferred	...	31-8-26	...	To 1/16th Punjab Regiment.
—	...	—	...	Serving.
—	...	—	...	Serving.
Transferred	...	30-8-30	...	To 4/14th Punjab Regiment.
—	...	—	...	Commandant, 1929.—Serving.
—	...	—	...	Serving.

APPENDIX V

BRITISH OFFICERS WHO SERVED WITH THE BATTALION ON FIELD SERVICE, 1914-1919

Name and Unit.	*Date of Joining.*	*Date of Departure.*	*Remarks.*
Lieutenant-Colonel C. F. Dobbie 9th Infantry	15-8-14	30-10-14	Sick.
Lieutenant-Colonel H. L. Anderson 9th Infantry	15-8-14	27-10-14	Wounded ; died 30-10-14.
Captain G. A. Jamieson ... 9th Infantry	15-8-14	13-1-16	Wounded, 27-4-15. Rejoined, 14-11-15. Wounded, 13-1-16. Died of wounds.
Captain L. J. Jones ... 9th Infantry	15-8-14	28-10-14	Killed.
Captain G. B. C. Irvine ... 9th Infantry	15-8-14	21-4-17	Wounded, 28-10-14. Rejoined, 23-1-17. Wounded, 21-4-17. Died of wounds, 15-5-17.
Captain R. W. Gaskell ... 9th Infantry	15-8-14	23-11-14	Prisoner of war.
Captain H. Etlenger ... 9th Infantry	15-8-14	27-4-15	Died of wounds.
Captain G. D. Martin ... 9th Infantry	15-8-14	21-1-17	Staff ; rejoined 24-4-17. Staff, 27-7-17.
Captain E. V. Wills, ... 9th Infantry.	15-8-14	23-11-14	Wounded.
Lieutenant R. D'A. S. Banks 9th Infantry	15-8-14	21-4-17	Killed.
Lieutenant J. C. D. Mullaly 9th Infantry	15-8-14	27-10-14	Prisoner of war.
Lieutenant H. Wade ... 9th Infantry	15-8-14	28-10-14	Killed.
Lieutenant B. W. Browning 9th Infantry	15-8-14	9-3-17	Wounded. Accidentally wounded, 26-11-15 ; rejoined 1-2-17.
Major H. A. Carleton ... 90th Punjabis	12-11-14	9-5-15	Wounded.
Captain E. H. F. Aphthorpe 90th Punjabis	12-11-14	23-11-14	Wounded.
Lieutenant G. Balfour ... 98th Infantry.	16-11-14	12-8-15	Rejoined own unit.
Lieutenant Fletcher ... 97th Infantry	17-11-14	23-11-14	Prisoner of war.
Captain G. Mortimer ... 10th Jats.	17-11-14	23-11-14	Killed.
Captain C. H. Jardine ... 96th Berar Infantry	8-12-14	26-7-16	Rejoined own unit.
Lieutenant A. M. Taylor 1st Brahmins	8-12-14	18-3-15	Transferred.
Lieutenant Fasken ... 95th Infantry	10-12-14	4-6-15	Transferred.

Name and Unit.	*Date of Joining.*	*Date of Departure.*	*Remarks.*
Captain Dempster ... 35th Sikhs	10-12-14	20-12-14	Wounded. Died as a prisoner of war.
Captain G. E. Cavendish 97th Infantry	14-12-14	22-12-14	Died of wounds.
Major F. W. Thomas ... 44th Merwara Infantry	27-12-14	13-1-16	Wounded, 9-5-15. Rejoined as C.O., 4-1-16. Died of wounds, 27-1-16.
Captain W. H. D. Wilson 1st Brahmins	1-1-15	4-3-15	Transferred.
Lieutenant A. H. Neale ... 1st Brahmins	1-1-15	9-7-15	Transferred.
Captain Kirkwood ... 97th Infantry	6-3-15	27-4-15	Wounded.
Captain E. J. Burdett ... 11th Rajputs	9-2-15	4-6-15	Transferred.
Major O'Reily ... ... 63rd Infantry	30-3-15	9-4-15	Transferred.
Captain N. H. H. Ralston 9th Infantry.	22-4-15	9-5-15	Wounded.
2/Lieutenant B. Hayfield I.A.R.O.	10-5-15	9-7-15	Transferred.
2/Lieut. E. Cameron Ker	12-5-15	7-1-16	Wounded.
Major F. C. Samborne-Palmer 8th Rajputs	19-5-15	30-12-15	Transferred.
2/Lieutenant W. H. Morrison I.A.R.O.	27-7-15	6-4-16	Wounded.
2/Lieutenant F. C. Roberts I.A.R.O.	27-7-15	—	Wounded, 13-1-16 and 21-4-17; returned with unit.
Captain H. H. Smith ... 9th Infantry	28-7-15	—	Returned with Unit.
2/Lieutenant F. L. Woledge	28-7-15	1-2-19	Transferred.
2/Lieutenant S. E. Grundy I.A.R.O.	29-8-15	18-11-15	Sick.
2/Lieutenant P. M. McSwiney I.A.R.O.	29-8-15	23-9-16	Sick.
Lieutenant W. B. Tyndall 7th Rajputs	5-2-16	19-3-16	Sick.
Lieutenant H. Newman ... I.A.R.O.	5-2-16	25-6-18	Transferred.
Lieut. H. J. M. Flaxman... I.A.R.O.	15-2-16	16-1-18	Transferred.
Lieutenant-Colonel H. G. Bell 27th Punjabis	2-3-16	6-3-16	Sick.
Captain H. L. Morris ... 17th Infantry	2-3-16	2-5-16	Sick.
2/Lieutenant W. R. Moll 9th Infantry	30-3-16	7-7-16	Sick.
2/Lieutenant P. R. Solly ... I.A.R.O.	20-5-16	2-6-16	Transferred.
Lieutenant C. O. Mosse ... 120th Rajputana Infantry	25-5-16	2-6-16	Transferred.
Major A. del Faunce ... 9th Infantry.	21-8-16	24-10-16	Sick.

Name and Unit.	Date of Joining.	Date of Departure.	Remarks.
2/Lieutenant E. A. Stead 35th Sikhs	29-9-16	6-1-18	Transferred.
Lieutenant-Colonel Roos-malecocq 8th Gurkhas	3-10-16	9-10-16	Sick.
2/Lieutenant K. M. Ross... I.A.R.O.	6-10-16	9-10-16	Sick.
2/Lieutenant H. B. Walling I.A.R.O.	25-10-16	27-2-18	Transferred.
2/Lieutenant D. F. Hubert I.A.U.L.	7-11-16	14-3-17	Killed.
2/Lieutenant L. H. Rodwell I.A.R.O.	4-12-16	—	Returned with Unit.
2/Lieutenant C. T. Smith I.A.R.O.	11-12-16	27-8-17	Transferred.
Captain L. P. Brotherton 3rd Brahmins	28-12-16	29-1-17	Transferred.
2/Lieutenant I. A. M. Weatherall I.A.R.O.	24-4-17	2-3-19	Transferred.
2/Lieutenant N. P. Townley I.A.R.O.	5-5-17	19-2-18	Transferred.
Lieutenant H. W. Bowsfield I.A.R.O.	9-5-17	15-9-18	Transferred.
Major P. A. Maxwell ... 3rd Brahmins	5-6-17	6-10-17	Transferred.
Captain G. Ireland ... 13th Rajputs	27-10-17	—	Returned with Unit.
Captain W. de L. Passey... 113th Infantry	31-10-17	13-1-18	Transferred.
Lieutenant A. S. Mathewman 94th Russells Infantry	7-1-18	27-1-18	Transferred.
2/Lieutenant J. D. Malcolm I.A.R.O.	27-2-18	—	Returned with Unit.
2/Lieutenant D. W. B. Owens I.A.R.O.	27-2-18	—	Returned with Unit.
Lieutenant E. M. Carter ... I.A.R.O.	27-5-18	27-1-19	Transferred.
Lieutenant A. H. Bevan I.A.R.O.	27-5-18	21-9-18	Transferred.
2/Lieutenant R. A. Collett I.A.R.O.	13-6-18	25-6-18	Transferred.
2/Lieutenant P. C. J. Leigh I.A.R.O.	18-10-18	—	Returned with Unit.
2/Lieutenant J. Murphy ... I.A.R.O.	19-10-18	5-2-19	Demobilized.
Lieutenant W. S. Holden	23-10-18	9-2-19	Transferred.
Lieutenant A. H. Butler I.A.R.O.	9-1-19	28-1-19	Transferred.
Lieutenant N. MacDonald I.A.R.O.	27-1-19	10-3-19	Transferred.
Captain G. Brock ... I.M.S.	15-8-14	28-12-14	Sick.
Captain W. O. Wright ... I.M.S.	1-2-15	4-6-15	Transferred.
Lieutenant M. Das, I.M.S.	4-4-15	—	Returned with Unit.
2/Lieutenant Cooke ...	3-10-14	4-6-15	Interpreter.

APPENDIX VI

LIST OF UNITS WHO SUPPLIED REINFORCEMENTS TO THE BATTALION IN THE FIELD

Depot 9th Bhopal Infantry.
17th Infantry.
89th Punjabis.
1st Brahmins.
21st Punjabis.
96th Berar Infantry.
4th Rajputs.
18th Infantry.
11th Rajputs.
5th Light Infantry.
16th Rajputs.
19th Punjabis.
8th Infantry.
26th Punjabis.
7th Rajputs.
Burma Military Police.

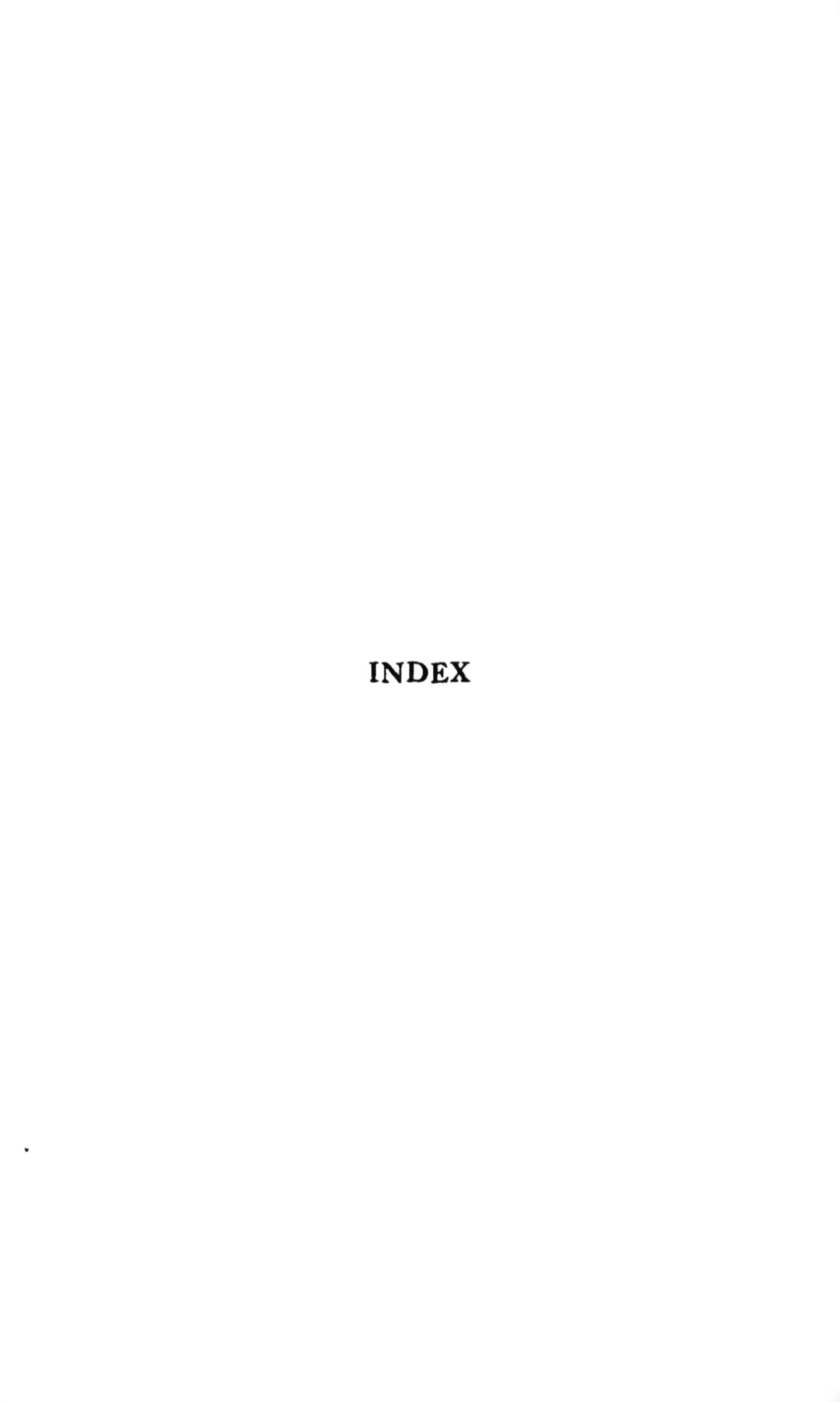

INDEX

INDEX

www.ingramcontent.com/pod-product-compliance
Ingram Content Group UK Ltd.
Pitfield, Milton Keynes, MK11 3LW, UK
UKHW041847190726
13854UKWH00002B/762

9 781845 741969